A Walk in the Park

A Walk in the Park

A Narration of the History of Riverside Park and the Surrounding Areas of Delran, New Jersey

HAROLD KLINGLER SR.

Copyright © 2017 Hal Klingler Sr.

All rights reserved. No part of this book may be used or reproduced by any means, graphic, electronic, or mechanical, including photocopying, recording, taping or by any information storage retrieval system without the written permission of the author except in the case of brief quotations embodied in critical articles and reviews.

Archway Publishing books may be ordered through booksellers or by contacting:

Archway Publishing
1663 Liberty Drive
Bloomington, IN 47403
www.archwaypublishing.com
1 (888) 242-5904

Because of the dynamic nature of the Internet, any web addresses or links contained in this book may have changed since publication and may no longer be valid. The views expressed in this work are solely those of the author and do not necessarily reflect the views of the publisher, and the publisher hereby disclaims any responsibility for them.

Any people depicted in stock imagery provided by Thinkstock are models, and such images are being used for illustrative purposes only.
Certain stock imagery © Thinkstock.

ISBN: 978-1-4808-3979-3 (sc)
ISBN: 978-1-4808-3980-9 (e)

Library of Congress Control Number: 2016918794

Print information available on the last page.

Archway Publishing rev. date: 3/30/2017

Contents

Introduction ix

Part 1:   The Early Years 1
Part 2:   Burlington County 4
Part 3:   The Grist mills 6
Part 4:   The Bridges 7
Part 5:   A Township Divided 9
Part 6:   Family History 11
Part 7:   The Great Depression 13
Part 8:   St. Mihiel Dr. 18
Part 9:   Chester Ave. 42
Part 10: River Drive 60
Part 11: Stewart Ave. 70
Part 12: Alden Ave. 102
Part 13: Norman Ave. 122
Part 14: Cambridge 131
Part 15: Rt.130 139
Part 16: Bridgeboro 144

Acknowledgements 153

I Dedicated This Book to My Wife Elaine and Family

Introduction

When the Second World War ended, and the boys began to come home, the country went into a short lived recession. By 1950 business started to pick up and the demographics were changing rapidly. Realtors came in buying and selling building lots. Contractors were building single family homes, developers were scooping up large sections of land and the housing boom began. The first housing development started in the Cambridge area and was named Delcrest. As the building continued throughout Cambridge and along Chester Ave. a new street was added and named Greenwood Ave. This was the divided line between Riverside and Delran.

In and around the same time Pancoast Boulevard in the Fairview section was also added and lead to many smaller streets and houses in Fairview. Then, another large housing development on Haines Mill Rd. named Millside Heights. Since the developers crossed over Rt. 130 the farm land became vulnerable and Bridegboro was gobbled up right before our eyes. Today, there's not a farm to be had.

As the developers built their version of modern living, they bestowed each area with a name, the most well known Tenby Chase. During this period of time each section received a new identity like Delcrest, Tenby Chase, Hunters Glen, and so on.

Now that the 60's were upon us, we acquired the Township name of Delran which derives from its birthplace at the Delaware River and the Rancocas Creek. "Riverside Park" is the only place in the township where the Delaware and the Rancocas touch its shore line.

When this land was acquired from the Haines family its starting point began at the flood gates near Dredge Harbor. The Stewart's Farm was the first to be purchased in 1916 and developed at this point in time; I cannot fine the developers name but after the streets were laid out, brick columns 30 inches square by 7 feet tall were erected with the names of each street. Over the years people took it on their own to remove them, but I'm proud to say that a few of our home owners keep the remaining two in good condition. You can see one in a photo at my grandfather's house at Alden Ave.

The two that remain are on Chester Ave. One is kept by Sissy and Rex Workman, the other is kept by Diana and Josh Dudek who are late comers but also involved in this community as officers of the Delran Historical Society.

After living here for a few years, you'll feel the spirit of what we call "The Park." I have said many times that when Chief Ockanickon waved his hand over this ground and sanctified it for his Unami Indian tribes men to plant and fish here, that the sanctification still lingers here today.

As you read on you will find many testimonies to this fact, that there is something here in "The Park" that grabs on to you and refuses to let go. When you visit Delran for the first time you'll notice signs denoting different housing developments which were added during the last few years; those seven foot columns I speak about were on each street corner along St Mihiel Drive and when they were removed, we lost our identity

Now you can see why I wrote this book. I was convinced by others that our identity must be preserved in the written word, this is exactly what I set out to do, and I hope I've accomplished.

Part 1
The Early Years

Let's go back a few centuries to the 1600's. The Lenni Lenape and the Unami Indian tribes occupied this part of central New Jersey which is now Burlington County. They liked this central part for the fact that it was a very short distance by foot from the Delaware River to the Atlantic Ocean.

The old path on the New Jersey side of the Delaware River began near Plum Point, not far from the foot of present Taylors Lane, and reaches across portions of Cinnaminson, Delran, Moorestown, Mt. Laurel, and Medford to approach the seacoast. Indians from both sides of the river used the trail for their annual journey to the sea.

The migration traditionally came in June after their maize was planted on the home grounds. Many of the natives, arriving at the seacoast in June, did not hurry back. Some of them remained until August or September setting a pattern that the white man was later to emulate. The mound of oyster and clamshells found along the coast by early colonists attest to the Indians visits, and to their duration.

This was not the only road across Jersey to the sea but it was the most used by the Indians. After a time the white settler had purchased more ground for farming and then, an early ferry was established in 1705 and known as Hopkins Ferry which was close to Plum Point and the flood gates. The colonials traveled the old Indian road until about 1721, when the "road to Chester," now known as Riverton Road, was laid out to accommodate inland travel.

The old road gradually fell to disuse and only by inference can its winding course be estimated today. This portion of the Delaware River and the Rancocas Creek was very good for fishing trapping hunting and farming. For these very same reasons the Europeans came to this area and settle here between 1678 and 1692.

The Swedish farmers moved down into the southern part of New Jersey and even down into Delaware, except for two families, who established farms along a small tributary fed by the Delaware River, traveling south which became known as Swedes Run.

The early colonist was predominantly English, Swedish and French. In this area, later known as Delran, four names are considered the pioneers. The family of John and Grace Hollinshead who came to this country in 1678 and purchased 550 acres of land, and Thomas Hackney, whose daughter Agnes married John Hollinshead Jr., and Thomas Hooton, a tallow chandler of Black Friars England, who purchased 500 acres near what, is now known as Bridgeboro in 1682.

The principal landowner at this period was Matthew Allen who bought 3200 acres of land in 1680; his land comprised much of the present Delran Township. Matthew Allen married the Widow Conarroe who, with her sons came to this country in 1680. They left France and went to England where they traveled in the tide of Quaker migration to the new world. By deed of gift on May 12, 1683, Allen transferred 500 acres along the Delaware River to his stepson Jacob Conarroe and another 500 acres on Swedes Run to his stepson Isaac. They also had a younger son Daniel.

Another early resident was Henricus Jacobsen Falconbre who came from Denmark to New Jersey prior to the time of the Quaker settlement. Because his name was so hard to pronounce, they gave him the name Henry Jacobs. Thus his survey of 1681 reads: Memorandum of survey for Henry Jacobs of 200 acres of land on the Southside of and along Rancocas Creek at the mouth of a small branch.

Here you can see the landowners of Delran Township and the

amount of land they purchased. First to the last, John Hollinshead in 1678 purchased 550 acres. Matthew Allen in 1680 purchased 3200 acres. Thomas Hooton in 1682 purchased 500 acres. This is a total of 4,250 acres. (640 acres to a square. mile) For all practical purposes this is the size of Delran today.

This Danish settler Henry Jacobs had learned the local Indian tongue. As early as 1677 he was employed by the Quaker Commissioners of West New Jersey, to act as an interpreter in negotiations with the natives for deeds of three large tracts of land, between midstream of the Rancocas Creek and midstream of Timber Creek, and grew out of these negotiations. The Indian deed for lands in the Delran and adjacent vicinity was signed September 10, 1677.

The ancient deed was signed by the Commissioners on the one hand and by the marks of Indian chieftains Katanas, Sokappie, Enequato, Rennowighwan, and Jackickon. The considerations were: Thirty blankets, 150 pounds of powder, thirty guns, thirty kettles, 7 anchors of brandy, 36 rings, 100 fish hooks, 1 gross of pipes, 10 spoonful of paint, 30 each of small bows, bells, knives, forks, bracelets, tobacco, 'toungs' flints, looking glasses, Jews harps, and awl, thirty pair of stockings, thirty pair of 'scissors' and 46 fordone and Duffelds- whatever they were (N.J. Vol. B early deeds). During the Quaker migration of 1675-1682 the land of central New Jersey was known as West Jersey and was divided into "Tenths" and later this system of Tenths was set aside in favor of a "County system."

Part 2

Burlington County

This central part of New Jersey became Burlington County, and with its inception began to incorporate townships into the county. The town of Bridgeboro was established in 1838 and became incorporated into the county as part of Delran Township in 1880. If you happen to be checking out water tanks in different townships, you'll notice the names and dates, and sometimes a slogan, is proudly displayed honoring these townships. Check out your water tank.

The Delran water tank has the date in which it was incorporated into the County of Burlington in 1880. Around 1692 this area of Chester Township included the area of what would become the future of Riverside, Delran, Riverton, Palmyra, Cinnaminson and Moorestown.

In the 1730's a ferry was used to cross the Rancocas creek connecting Burlington to Salem, along the Burlington Salem Road. The dock for the ferry was placed at the lower forks of the Rancocas Creek here in Delran.

New Jersey played a crucial role in getting members of the colonies to join together as one; they held a meeting in Burlington City along the waterfront and this Committee of Correspondence and Inquiry formed what was known as the "Committee of Nine" to act for the Colonies. Three of the nine members were from the city of Burlington. They later voted for a "Congress of Deputies" to take up the cause.

The County played a large role in the Revolutionary War. It became the major staging ground late in the war due to the fact that the British were landing troops along the Delaware River and also along the Atlantic, at Sandy Hook. One interesting note is the fact that 2000 Hessian troops at Mount Holly were kept busy during the Battle of Iron Works Hill, giving Gen. George Washington time to win the Battle of Trenton. There was also the famous battle of Assunpink Bridge, which is now Mercer County. Burlington County was quite large in the 1700's. It extended north up into Mercer County and east to the shore and south to Gloucester and west to the Delaware River.

This was the cross roads of the Revolutionary War. There were 300 battles fought here in Burlington County. If you think about it, the British had to transport their troops by ship from the Atlantic, into Sandy Hook, or up through the Delaware River. One of the main troop crossings of the Rancocas Creek was in what would become Delran, at the far end of Bridgeboro near Moorestown. At the time there was a ferry at Old Salem Road operated by the Hollinshead family. As far as the war goes they were impartial to the Continentals and the British. The ferry continued operating throughout the war.

Part 3

The Grist mills

During this time period Borton's grist mill was established along Swedes Run in 1750, and was later sold to Jacob Haines who rebuilt the old grist mill in 1805. At his death the mill and property descended down three generations over the years. Till finally in 1879 Horace Haines, the last owner, added a steam powered engine and new machinery, and including new roller mills instead of the traditional water wheel powered gristmills making it a first-class flour mill.

The property remained in the Haines family throughout the century. This property was later owned by Kendal and Lasklockey who were partners in a dairy farm, and later became Millside Farms. When the Millside industrial park was being built behind the present day Delran Municipal building, during the excavating two large mill stones were found belonging to the old Haines grist or flour mill and are responsible for the naming of Haines Mill Road.

This unearthing of the millstones gave light to the possibility that just maybe, the new mill not needing large amounts of water, could have been built upstream; but then again while dismantling the old plant, they could have rolled these millstones across Burlington pike, and as the landscape gradually slopes downward, the momentum of these millstones could have carried them 100 yards, or where they were found when they fell over. One will never know. Later they were shipped off to a buyer in Virginia. People like to bury these millstones edge wise in the ground and place their house number on the face of the top extruding half.

Part 4

The Bridges

In a section of Delran, close to the Moorestown border a little upstream from the old ferry a covered bridge was built in 1793 that crossed the Rancocas Creek just below the forks at the old Burlington Salem Road, and was later bought up by the Toll-Bridge Company. A new bridge was erected by T. Baker in 1838.

Around this time the name of Bridgeborough was being used at this site. Finally in late1838 they decided to change the name to Bridgeboro. Another bridge was built across the Rancocas Creek at Rt.25 in 1927 and now the latest bridge in 1984 which is an over pass.

At this same sight in 1740 the Post Rider delivered mail across the Rancocas. The Camden and Amboy Railroad helped with the growth of the Riverfront communities. The area at the time was part of Chester Township, and later Cinnaminson Township which was incorporated in 1860.

In 1880 a document that states in part, that Charles Haines sold a portion of his property from the flood gates by the Delaware River in a South easterly direction parallel with the Public Road leading by Taylor Station on the Camden and Amboy Railroad to New Albany in a straight line to the Northern boundary line of the Township of Chester, which is now Moorestown. All the parts lying east of the said line shall constitute and be known as the Township of Delran. There were more towns carved up into what is now known as the Riverfront

Communities. In 1893 the State Assembly voted to offset Palmyra and Riverton from Cinnaminson Township, and in 1894 they voted to offset Riverside from Delran Township, turning all these towns into townships of their own.

Part 5

A Township Divided

Delran Township became divided in to four parts up to 1967, Bridgeboro, Fairview, Cambridge, and Riverside Park. The purpose was for Riverside Post Office to separate the mail for the Carriers in each section of Delran. The boundary lines seem to be arbitrary at the time but most of the residents considered Bridgeboro to be on the North bound sides of Route 130 to the border of Moorestown, and on the South bound side of Route 130 was considered Fairview which was mostly farms and also The United Episcopal Church.

There was a time when both sides of Rt. 130 were known as Fairview. Partly down Chester Ave Fairview came to an end, with Riverside Township on the eastside and Delran Township to the west with more farms down to the railroad tracks, from the railroad tracks down to the Delaware River and Rancocas Creek and as far down to Taylors Lane was considered Riverside Park.

Going west on the opposite side of the tracks over to Swedes Run was Kentzingers Farm and then the section named Cambridge. This is how Delran was divided up in the early days. The population of Cambridge and Riverside Park totaled about 700 people. The Fairview section was sparsely populated with a few farmers and their families. Bridgeboro was mostly farms with a population of about 400.

Let's start at Rt.130 and go north along Chester Ave. Here we find Millside Farms and on the opposite side, a large section of ground which is now the home of Holy Cross High School. Then John Frecks farm of 31 acres, which is now the Chester Ave Middle School, and then back over to the left side, there was Casper Alzheimer's farm of 12 acres, then Andy Kentzinger's farm of 75 acres, which continued down to the railroad tracks.

Now we head west over to the Cambridge area. On the far side of Cambridge, over to Swedes Run, there was a farm owned by the Harris family. Charlie was the last surviving member of the Harris family farm. He was an old fashioned farmer and a good guy.

We have Quaker meeting houses, and Friends Schools here in the neighboring towns of Riverton and Moorestown. I think we were very fortunate to follow up with some of the Quaker traditions. We can look across the Delaware River from here in Delran, and see the great city skyline of Philadelphia Pennsylvania, where William Penn stands atop city hall. I'm reminded that the Penn Charter William Pen signed, was his inheritance from his father back in England, and was the precursor of a nation yet to come. We were always proud to be a suburb of Philadelphia. In the late 1800's Riverside was part of Delran Township, a resort town for Philadelphians, and quite a few came here and liked it. Some came and stayed. I guess my great grandparents liked it or I'd still be in Philadelphia.

Part 6

Family History

My great-great grandfather Francis Augustus Klingler and my great-great grandmother Christiana Klingler along with their seven children left Alsace Lorrain which was on the boarder of Germany and France to come to America. They boarded the ship R.D. Shepherd at La Havre France, and arrived at a N.Y. Harbor in 1847. It was quite obvious why they were leaving their home for the new world across the Atlantic; Europe was in turmoil, freedom of religion was hard to come by, and there was one war after another.

When they did arrive, they then traveled by train to the city of Philadelphia, Pennsylvania where they settled down and found work. For the most part they were in the shoe making business and had a store on Market St. Then the Civil War began and in 1861 my great grandfather, Matthew Klingler, enlisted in the 71st. Pennsylvania Volunteer Inf. Co. A. He served throughout the war, including the Battle of Gettysburg as a Surgeons Steward. His brother, Francis, enlisted in the U.S.Navy and served at Port Royal South Carolina.

While the war raged on, the family moved their shoe business to Tasker Avenue. After Matthew returned home from the war, he married Amelia Kampen and moved to Baring Street where he continued to work and raise 9 children.

When Matthew passed away, the family moved to Hancock St. in

Riverside, N.J. in 1878, which included his wife Amelia K. Klingler head of the house, and three children Joseph, Paul, and Henrietta.

My great-great grandmother Christiana Klingler moved in with the family at Hancock St. sometime later. Her Death and Burial Index shows she died on March 12, 1892 in Delran, Burlington County, New Jersey. At that time, Riverside, N.J. was part of Delran Township.

Amelia's son Paul M. Klingler married Mary Joseph of Riverside, Mary's father, Charlie Joseph, and her mother Anna (Kiliian) Joseph was from Riverside.

Paul M.Klingler and Mary Joseph Klingler raised five sons in Riverside Charles, Paul, (Francis), Albert, and Julius, all members of St. Peter's Church in Riverside.

My father, Francis Klingler was born in Riverside in 1903. Then the family moved to Philadelphia. After a number of years they moved back to Delran where they lived for the rest of their lives, with the exception of my father and mother, who lived for a brief time at 5th and Chester Ave. in Riverside, N.J. where I was born on January 2, 1928. By the time I was seven years old we were back in Delran, to stay.

Part 7

The Great Depression

Back in the 20's and even into the 30's being born at home was the job of a midwife and in Riverside. Helen Daehne was one who delivered quite a few babies.

By the age of five I remember going to Carrol Street School. There was a large park across the street which had a fountain and some type of figure in the center. Today at Fifth and Chester Ave. there's an athletic field which is totally encompassed with chain link fence. At the time we lived there, the AA field had a six foot wooden plank fence all the way around.

Our home had a small flat roof on the back of the house, and when the Riverside fire company had donkey baseball games to raise money, my sister and I would climb out the bedroom window onto that flat roof to watch the games. It was fun watching them hit the ball, hop on the donkey and ride around the bases.

We also had very good neighbors. The Siegfried family lived next door with two daughters and a son and next to them the Myers family with two daughters and a son. My mother and father also had two daughters and a son, (yours truly). Now all of us kids, being close in age, were going to school together, playing games after school like hopscotch and running tag to mention a few. It was only natural to become very friendly with them and their parents. The backyards were large, which gave us plenty of room to play. I have to mention their names even if it s just for my own satisfaction and therefore I'll start with the oldest down to the youngest. The Siegfried's were Helen then Dorothy and their brother Gus. The Myers was Irma then grace, and Fred. They had a daughter Ruth born much later. Then there was our family, Eleanor, myself and Shirley, and at this date 2012 there are three left out of nine, Helen (Siegfried) Sharpley, Dorothy (Siegfried) Bart, and I.

I have two younger brothers, Francis and Wayne that were born much later and are doing fine. It's sad when I think of our siblings that are no longer with us but there is still that heartfelt feeling that I'm thankful for and the friendship between all of us that lingers on and on.

My father, as a builder, built our first home in Riverside and it wasn't long before the 1929 stock market crash came along and our house was repossessed by the bank. Before going into the building trade, my father had already finished the machinist trade in the family machine shop. We moved to a rental house on Roland St. in Riverside Park, N.J. I was too young to know that Riverside Park was a post office address in Delran N.J. It was a very interesting place to grow up and now as an Octogenarian, I'd like to take you back and paint a picture of the town that not only lives in my memory, but also in my heart.

At the age of seven living on Roland St. in Riverside Park, the town consisted of a mere three (3) blocks square, which ran parallel from St. Mihiel Drive to the last street on the banks of the Rancocas Creek, which was another three (3) blocks. On the west side of Norman Ave. there was a ball field, an unfinished road and a house at the end which is Reserve Ave. It then continued further west along River Road down to Taylors Lane.

You have to realize this was 1935, the height of the Great Depression, and I had no idea what this was all about. We were not exactly poor, but a lot of people were. At this young age it didn't seem to have much of an impact on my life. I did notice that my mother and father were struggling to make ends meet, especially with three children; that is, my two sisters and I, my oldest sister Eleanor was (9) going on (10). She had no choice but to grow up before her time, she looked after my younger sister and me, also thanks to my grandmother who helped us through this struggling time.

On occasion my mother would let me pull the wagon all the way to Riverside to pick up our rations from the municipal building on Scott Street and then to Wills market, and then back up Pavilion Ave. to the paper store where my mother would buy me a penny's worth of candy. Oh, yes, I'll always remember that wagon and a penny's worth of candy. We went up to Riverside and when we returned it was always down to the Park. Riverside was north and the Park was south, it was kind of related to Rt. 130. When we unloaded the wagon there was usually a large can of cabbage with a trace of ham somewhere in the mix, a pound of lard, and some bread and a small ration of milk. There seemed to be a shortage of everything.

Most homes had coal fired furnaces and you had to sign up for a delivery which was a quarter ton of coal. You had to make it last through the winter by also using wood. When I talked to other people that lived through the Great Depression they also remember the lard sandwich. They consisted of one slice of bread spread with lard, sprinkled with salt and pepper. At the time I was so hungry it tasted like ice cream.

My father was out of work for a short time and yes, my mother was lucky to find a job working for Mr. Fairbrother at the paper store in Riverside. She made $1.00 a day, five days a week, which was big money at the time. After some time my father found a job at Four Mile Colony. The State was building new housing for the blind and disabled. When these building were finished they invited the builders and their families to an open house celebration.

The buildings were constructed of red brick, with a beautiful interior of tile floors and spacious rooms for different types of activities. At the time of our visit, the partially blind were weaving baskets of numerous colors; it was a great experience and a wonderful day in all.

The Great Depression continued on, and a lot of people were out of work, but we survived for the fact that my father had a great work ethic. He later worked two part time jobs, one with his brother Paul in the machine shop on Stewart Ave. and the other with my mother's Uncle Howard Wills from Delanco, N.J.

Howard hired my father to build houses at Sea Isle, New Jersey along the shore. My father traveled back and forth in his used model T Ford. He had an unusual way of starting that old model T, that is, if someone was watching. There were no starters on these cars back then. They came with a crank handle that you would insert through a hole into the front of the car. There was a key or switch to turn the ignition on and off. The first thing to do was to leave the ignition off. There were two leavers on the steering column one was the throttle, the other the spark. He would adjust these leavers to a starting position, then go to the front of the car and grab the handle and crank the engine over twice, then bring the crank handle up slow until it was on what was called died center. Then he would go back and turn the steering wheel until the front tire touched the crank handle, then turn the key on, go back and kick the front tire which hit the crank handle pushing it off center and spinning the engine so it would start. This was a routine that was setup waiting for the right person to come along.

There was very little radio and no TV naturally; this was part of the self made entertainment. It wasn't unusual to find a house party on the weekend. There were lots of entertainers of all kinds at our Aunt Anna's boarding house in Riverside. The room at the back of the house was very large and it was the full width of the house, serving as a kitchen and also the entertainment room.

On Saturday night there were tap dancers, magicians, poets, comedians and musicians. It was like Ted Mack, Milton Berle, or Saturday Night Live before its time.

I can still remember when at home, sitting around the dining room table listening to one of President Roosevelt's fire side chats. We had a second hand radio which operated from dry cell batteries, and a headset with a unique way of amplifying the sound. I always admired my father's ingenious way to solve a problem. He placed a large glass bowl in the center of the dining room table, then with the headset on, he would tune the radio. When the station came in clear he would place the headset into the glass bowl, and told us all to lean forward with our ear close to the bowl. It was amazing how this amplified the sound of President Roosevelt's voice coming from that glass bowl.

We lived on Roland St. for about two and a half years and then moved to #10 Stewart Ave. I still remember that house on Roland St. being sold to Charlie Stellwag for $500. He worked as a proof reader for the Philadelphia Inquirer which was a highly skilled occupation at the time. Still, $500 dollars was a lot of money back then. The Stellwag family fit right into this place we call The Park. At this young age I started to get acquainted with the people and the businesses of this small section of Delran Township.

Part 8

St. Mihiel Dr.

Let's start at the corner of Chester Ave. and St. Mihiel Dr. The Dipsey Doodle was a sandwich shop operated by Margaret Maguire. She tried to change the name but it never worked out, it would always be the Dipsey Doodle.

There were different businesses in and out of here for a number of years. Ray Colonna had his Barber Shop here. He also lived here in one of the rental houses on Chester Ave. He taught his nephew Phil to cut hair at this shop and in time Phil opened his own Barber Shop in Palmyra. Later Ray moved to the family shop in Delanco, and then to Beverly. The family shop in Delanco is still owned and operated by Ray's nephew, Vince Colonna. While Ray lived here in the Park he played music in the clubs and bars as a guitarist. He loved music and shared some of his techniques with me at the time. It seems like just yesterday when Ray and I talked about music and how we played guitars.

A family named Swain opened up this sandwich shop and named it the "Dipsey Doodle," it was a regular hang out for the kids, it had two tables with chairs and a pinball machine, Margaret treated all of us kids like we were her own. Some of the guys who had cars would park them down the street and walk up with their girlfriends. Others would meet their friends there, and if there was a table open they would sit inside and have a sandwich and a soda and listen to the jukebox; others would just hang around out front and talk about cars, motorcycles or movies.

It was like the television series Happy Day's and everyone got along. Yes there were guys who came from out of town that fit in with the rest of us; their cars motorcycles or trucks were the big talk. You may remember these names; Milky Winters, Zip Caruso, Don Lindh, Bucket Head Miller, Ed Shinn, Don Shafer. The few of us who are still around have fond memories of Edith Marshall & Albert (ducky) Pippit. By the way this is now Milanese Pizza.

Traveling along the front street over to Stewart Ave. there were three more businesses. The first was a Beauty Shop operated by Alberta Morrison where most women in the area frequented. This is where they got the latest news, and if you did something wrong, the next time your mother came home from Alberta's you were in for it. I guess this was the sign of a close knit community which kept the young people from straying too far out of the norm. If you think about it, what an asset this was to the community. Alberta kept the women beautiful and the young people in line.

Dale Pfeifer, his wife Betty had five sons, Wayne, Dale Jr, Danny, Donald and David moved next to Alberta. Previously they lived on Norman Avenue just a few houses up from the old Mansion.

This is where tragedy struck one summer's day in the early 50's. Their young son Wayne disappeared; He was eight years old and nowhere to be found. Our one police officer William (Dur) Horner began a missing person's investigation.

The fire company was out searching every possible lead they could drum up. Two days went by without any sightings, ironically the carnival was in town and about to leave, when Officer William Horner informed them that they had to remain in town until his investigation was finished.

Then on the third day the "First Responders" arrived and began a search along the water ways at the Riverside Marina. A hard hat diver namely Frannie Schaffer walked into the water where there were steel tracks for lowering boats into the harbor. After a few minutes he found Wayne's body tangled in some old cables. Finally the search was over and although it was a relief in one sense of the word, it was a tragedy in another.

At this new address the family seemed to have some kind of stability in their life and as time went on the boys grew up and went their own way. Later some became Firemen and in time Dale Sr. became Chief of the Fire Company, Betty joined the ladies Auxiliary and Dale also served as Mayor of Delran. Even today when I talk to one of the boys, I can see the sadness in their demeanor for the loss of their young brother.

Irene Tinsdale operated a small mom & pop store at #9 St. Mihiel Dr. We called her Tinney. She was a great lady. Her husband Harry built this house with a store front for Irene and he ran a huckster business around town until he passed away at a young age. She kept on operating the store until she sold the property and the business to her niece, Lydia Boenitsch. It was a cozy store that had a counter with a register, a Deli counter, a candy and ice cream counter, and a gumball machine. Behind the counters were shelves with canned goods and bread; on top of the counters were Tasty Cakes and some other treats.

Mrs. Tinsdale was a trusting woman; she had a book on the counter were you could mark down what you bought. Many times people would just leave the money on the counter. Times were tough and she recognized that some of us needed attention, and at different times she would say, "Let's have lunch," and a handful of us kids would head for the kitchen which was right behind the store itself. This was a two story house. The doorways were pretty much in line, and you could stand in the store at the Deli counter and look right through the dining room into the kitchen. She could make the sandwiches pour the milk and keep an eye on the store. People were so trusting back then.

Lydia Boenitsch, Irene's niece, was of the same makeup. Everyone loved Lydia. She had one son John Jr. and a husband, John Sr., who was blind and a store to operate. Her brother-in-law Harry, John's Brother, helped out when he could. Before she came to Riverside Park she owned and operated a small store in Delanco and began to raise foster children. You would think that was enough to handle, but not for Lydia. She added a few more children after moving to the Park. As far as I can tell she raised 9 foster children, and one of these, five year old Harvey, drowned at Olympia lakes; so young, so sad. I still see some of them now and then; I have pictures of Jackie and Rita Keane, in a Palmyra High School year book. They went to school with my brother Francis. There are just two living in the house at #9 St. Mihiel Dr. Lydia's son John owns and operates the Flying Feather farm on the corner of Haines Mill & Bridgeboro Rd. along with his daughters and grandchildren. It's a picturesque farm stand with lots of fruits, vegetables and homemade pies.

The last business on the corner of St. Mihiel Dr. and Stewart Ave. was an auto repair shop owned and operated by Joe Raphael. It was also a Goodyear Tire agency. Before that it was Raphael & Johnson's General Tire. That partnership didn't last too long. Joe Raphael continued with the business and always had work for the young guys here in "The Park" who wanted to wash and polish cars, fix flat tires, and checking on batteries that were being charged.

During WWII tires were rationed. If you had a defense job, the township would issue you a ration slip to take to a local garage and purchase retread tires, and Joe would sell you vulcanized tires that were in stock for $5.00 each, and take your old tires and send them to a factory to be vulcanized. There was no such thing as new tires for civilians, only government cars and the armed force vehicles had new tires. When the vulcanized tires came back from the factory they were smooth, and that was one of my jobs, cutting new treads in that smooth surface of the tire. It was extra money in my pocket and I was glad to get it.

Another thing I always remembered was washing and polishing a car for a man from Riverton. I think his name was Richardson, and he had a 1928 Lincoln touring car with a V12 engine and an all aluminum body 1/8 inch in thickness. The body was painted canary yellow with a black roof and fenders. The inside had leather seats and hard wood trim around the doors and dashboard. It was a beauty and we always did a good job for Joe's customers.

Joe was another good community minded person, always willing to lend a helping hand when possible. He did have a humorous side at times. There was an undertaker from Riverside by the name of Bill Cunningham, and Joe would get someone's attention while the undertaker would walk up in back of them and begin to take a measurement with a 6ft tape. Joe would look to one side and the person would turn just as Bill Cunningham rolled up the tape. The whole act was in the timing and usually got a laugh.

Joe asked three of us musicians if he could be our manager, and if so, would we be willing to entertain the wounded soldiers at the Tilton hospital at Fort Dix N.J. We agreed and Joe set up the time, the date, and the program. His idea was to feature Lewie Anderson who was born without forearms. His upper arms ended where the elbow would normally be. We referred to them as his stumps, and he didn't mind that reference. He was about 3-1/2ft. tall and as a child he learned to crawl for a long time before he was able to stand. This birth defect left him with very little muscle in his legs, and consequently he stood in a crouch like a baseball catcher. Now with his fitted pants, this wasn't noticeable, but on occasions he could stand up straight to a height of a little over 4-1/2ft. This was one of those shock values he used on people at different times. Lewie and I were very good friends, and when he put out his right arm or stump and gave me a node, I would grab hold of his stump, and as I pumped up and down he would rise up about an inch or two each time. We would repeat this action until he was standing straight up. This is one of the tricks Joe would use in the act.

Joe asked us to dress like hillbillies and he would introduce us as the "Park Hillbilly Band". We agreed and when the evening came to leave for Fort Dix, John Smith picked up Lewie then me, and Joe Raphael last, who had the front passenger seat. Now if you can imagine, this was a rainy night and we're riding in a 1935 four door Buick sedan with a canvas roof, and right above Joe's head was a very slow leak and Joe was as bald as can be. Every once in a while a drop of rain water would land on Joe's head and it was hard not to laugh, but Joe took it with a good sense of humor while drying his head with his handkerchief.

We arrived at the Tilton Hospital, went in to a large auditorium and from the stage, there were more soldiers than I could count. Joe asked if someone would close the curtains and he told us where to stand. He instructed the person operating the curtain to open it just a little wider than the three of us. Joe then stepped out to center stage, greeted all the service men, and said he hoped they would enjoy the show. He announced the first song and stepped to the side of the stage. John Smith started the intro with the accordion, Lewie on the harmonica, and I sang the first song while playing guitar. Then Lewie with a solo on the harmonica and John played the Pennsylvania polka. John was a very good accordionist and he always got a lot of compliments. Lewie sang a popular country song and yodeled, and I mean yodeled. He taught me and many others how to yodel. He also did Swiss Alpine yodeling. There were quite a few southern boys in the hospital and when Lewie finished yodeling the place went wild with applause.

About that time Joe came back out on stage, walked over to Lewie and grabbed his hand so to speak and started to shake hands and as he did Lewie kept getting taller. Joe shouted "stop that" and began pushed down on Lewie's head. Lewie slowly shrunk down like letting air out of a tire. Now that Joe got everyone's attention he asked for a cigarette. Lewie slid a pack out of his pocket, grabbed it with his two stubs, and gave it a flip and a cigarette popped up. Joe took the cigarette and asked for a light. Lewie again went to his pocket, slid out a pack of matches and held them close to his hip, opened the cover, pulled out one match, slid it across the striker and gave Joe a light. Joe thanked Lewie and tossed a dime on the floor, Lewie bent over, grabbed the dime, and put it in his pocket, and with this the soldier boys all laughed and cheered with amazement. Joe knew they'd get a kick out of this entire show.

He turned back to the servicemen to talk about Lewie's disabilities. He said that Lewie was born this way and was determined to be a success in life and was about to get his driver's license. Joe wanted to show these soldiers not to let their disabilities hold them back. When we began to walk off stage, Joe called Lewie back. He said, "We have one more surprise for you boys. The curtains opened wide and two men pushed a piano to center stage. Joe said to Lewie." Play a song for the boys, Lewie" walked up to the piano and played a "snappy song" and walked off. He got such a round of applause that he had to play one more before the show ended and so he chose a hymn that he played many times in church. It seemed appropriate at the time. I think we had as much fun that night as the soldiers did. This was my first charity event. Little did I know there would be many more to come. This is also an example of Joe's patriotism and service to his country and community. When Joe retired from this business, the building sat idle for a short time.

Phil Crimmins opened the Riverside Ford Dealership here and in a few years he sold out to Paul Canton, and the dealership became Canton Ford, Paul Canton also had a used car lot near American Legion Drive in Riverside. Then in the early 60"s he sold the building to the L&M bakery and moved his dealership out to Rt. 130. in Delran. Not too long ago the L&M bakery celebrated 50 years selling and delivering great baked products, and it has become a land mark at St.Mihiel Dr. & Stewart Ave.

John Grob lived on the adjacent corner of Stewart Ave. across from Raphael's garage. He worked a lifetime for PSE&G, and served on the Township committee. When he passed away he left this house to his son and Daughter in-law Lester & Elva. The property was quite long probably 200ft or more, (We'll elaborate more about Lester when we go down Stewart Ave.). This house was a half double. The Bishop families lived in this half over the years. John Bishop was an automobile .mechanic and worked for Joe Raphael and years later his wife worked for L&M Bakery.

The next house was also a half double. Frank and Rose Cosky lived here with their two children, Stanley and Tom. In the other half lived my grandparents. Let me tell you about the Cosky family first. They lived here as long as my grandparents did in fact Rose still lives here. She made me promise not to tell her age. The only thing I can say is that she is a centenarian plus and I love her with all my heart.

Rose and Frank were very close friends with my mother and father. Our families grew closer as the years went by. Rose is small in stature but has a big heart and never complained about the life that fate had handed her. Her husband Frank and her son, Stanley, both suffered from alcoholism and Rose knew it was an illness long before the average person or neighbor could fathom what a devastating effect this has on a person's life. They also had a son, Thomas, who died at a young age.

Stanley and I were the same age and grew up in this neighborhood. His nick name was "Stosh" and he was always easy to get along with.

In later years Stosh and I both worked for the Campbell's Soup Co. in Camden N.J. I worked on the 5th floor in the Research Department. Stanley worked as a maintenance/machinist on the 3rd floor. He still had his problem with alcohol, and as time went on it just got worse. Finally the Campbell's Soup Company sent him away for treatment. I can't remember how long he was gone. It seemed like a couple of months.

Here is one of the many great things about the Campbell's Soup Co. They had a small parts department on the 3rd floor of the main plant in Camden. When an employee in maintenance came back to work after an illness, the supervisor would decide if they needed to spend some time in the small parts department. The worker would sit at a bench and assemble parts for different machinery. This is where Stanley worked for some time. The company did what they could for him but in time they had to let him go. It was evident that alcohol had consumed his body and in a short time he passed away. Rose and I talked about all of this and she was so grateful for what the Campbell's Soup Co. did for her son. She loved these two guys and suffered with them until they were gone. "Dear Rose I think you're a Saint".

My grandparents lived in the second half of this house. My step grandfather's name was changed to Paul Bruno when he came to America. He and his mother, father and one brother were French Canadians. He came down to Connecticut to pursue his trade as a tool & die maker; his real name was Neapolitan Onasine Brunea.

Now that he had finished his trade, he answered an advertisement for the Keystone Watchcase Co. in Riverside N.J. and landed the job. He and his first wife Ada moved here from Connecticut and never looked back. The tool & die maker trade was very lucrative at the time and so they bought this house where Paul lived the rest of his life. After a number of years Ada passed away, and Paul was alone in this big house.

Then as luck would have it a young man who had just lost his wife in child birth was looking for a room, his name, Dick Snow. To my step grandfather this was like having a son of his own. Dick Snow was a hard working auto mechanic. My grandmother Ella Richter lost her husband Charles Richter, who died from heart failure at a young age. She had two children, a daughter Helen and a son Charles Jr. whose nick name was Bud. She became a house keeper for Paul Brunea. He was a member at the Turners hall in Riverside and talked my grandmother into joining the auxiliary. Well, as you may know in a short time they were married. Helen is my mother and we lived just a block away. My uncle Bud was the youngest. Not long after my grandmother and my uncle Bud moved in with her new husband Paul. The Second World War came along and Bud and Dick Snow both joined the Navy. Now I had a grandfather but he was always Mr. Bruno to me. Now I had to get used to calling him Grandfather. I respected him; he was a good man and always took time to teach me valuable lessons of life. When pursuing the machinist trade he as a tool & die maker, gave me many great lessons in machine work that are still with me today.

Both of my grandfathers had passed on by the time I was two years old, so now I had the only grandfather I ever knew and he was great. Dick Snow and his son Dick Jr always seemed like family to me, we were very close. When Dick came home after the war he went to work for Max Berkowitz as an Auto Mechanic.

Charlie Rudolph lived next door and whenever I would saw up wood for my grandfather, Charlie would come over and teach me the proper way to handle that saw. These were long pieces of logs and sometimes Charlie would hold one end while I did the sawing. Neighbors were so helpful back then.

The Kelvey's lived in the next house. There were just three, Mrs. Kelvey and her daughter, Jean, and her son, Bob. Jean married John Wilkins. They lived at the lower end of Alden Ave. John passed away at a young age and Jean didn't last too many years after that. Bob married and move south. Like other people, once they move away we lose track of them.

Girt Hibbs and her son Harry lived in the next house. The husband was gone, which we'll never know the reason why the breakup. Girts maiden name was Stevenson and she was a sister to Harry Stevenson.

They grew up in Beverly where their father was a police officer. Her son, Harry, enlisted in the US Navy and served honorably during the Second World War.

The Hohmann family lived on the first corner of St. Mihiel Dr. and Alden Ave. They had five children. Listed in order there was Richard, Eleanor, Katy, John (John boy), and Emma. John boy and Emma were students at Cambridge School at the time I went there. We were very good friends and I got to know the family somewhat. John boy Hohmann had a good soul and knew the difference between right and wrong. I always thought his speech impediment was his only handicap. In today's thinking, he would have had a speech therapist and that could have made a world of difference. He had no problem in holding down his job at the Riverside Metal Co. He was a life time member of the Riverside Park Fire Company and he married and out lived two wives but has since left us, and our thoughts remain. Eleanor, Katie and Emma all married, Richard Hohmann became a teacher and taught Math & Science at Merchantville High School. Katie was the last one left in the family and just passed on 2011. The family all suffered in their later years from dementia, with the exception of Katie, she was sharp until her last days.

On the opposed corner lived Paul and Mary (Joseph) Klingler my grandparents and their five sons, Charlie, Paul, Francis, Albert and Julius. My grandfather was born and raised in Philadelphia and worked for Baldwin locomotive as a machinist and served his apprentice ship at the Spring Garden Institute in Philadelphia where he graduated with honors. I have his three certificates of accomplishments and a Bronze Medal in a felt case.

His parents were in the shoe business on Tasker Ave. in Philadelphia. My grandmother was born and raised in Riverside. Her father was Charlie Joseph and her mother, Amelia Killian Joseph, who came from a large Irish family. The Killians had a good number of daughters that lived in Riverside.

In 1930 my grandfather was killed in a train accident at Fairview St. Crossing in Riverside. At the time there was a small structure next to the track with one door and a sign at the top which read, "Watchman". When a train was on its way, the watchman would come out with a flag and stop anyone from crossing the tracks.

On this particular day the watchman left early and as my grandfather approached the crossing there was no watchman, no flag, and the structure for the watchman was blocking his view. Add to that the fact that my grandfather had lost his hearing. When he drove onto the track with his 1929 dodge sedan he was struck by the train. The car was later towed to the back of Gilberts Garage, alongside the Moose Hall which is now a parking lot for the Riverside Fire Department.

In a few years when all the boys were married and out of the house, my grandmother moved her mother Anna (Killian) Joseph, and father, Charlie Joseph, to St. Mihiel Dr. & Alden Ave, Riverside Park N.J. My great grandfather, Charlie Joseph was a civil war veteran. He served in Co. F, of the 20th Penn. Militia from the 19th of June to Aug 1863. He was discharged and then reenlisted as a Sgt. in Co. B. 19th Reg. of the Pennsylvania Cavalry from 1863 to 1866. He fought along with Maj. General Smith and Brig. General Grierson of the 118th Reg. in Nashville Tenn. and in 1864 he went to Franklin, Tenn. By 1866 he was discharged at New Orleans La. and when the war was over he came home to Riverside. He was born Oct. 8, 1847, died Mar. 4, 1934 and buried in Beverly National Cemetery, lot # 283. He spent the last years of his life in Riverside Park. N.J.

After my father finished building the Park Inn for Sam Zebrowski in 1939 Max Berkowitz asked my father to build a service station on St. Mihiel Dr. The property was right between the Park Inn and my grandmother's house. My father agreed to take the job but needed the plans for the size of the building, how many bays for car repair, and the size of the office. He also asked if there was going to be living quarters on the premises. When they came to an agreement my father made the drawing and a material list and asked Max if he would order the material as the job progressed.

This was in 1940 and my father was in the process of building our home on Alden Ave. I'll never forget helping him and learning valuable lessons of the building trade. I was 12 years old and worked with my father after school and on weekends. Sometimes it would be getting dark and there was just a little bit more to do, so I would hold a kerosene lamp close enough to the job so my father could finish for the day.

When we got back to #10 Stewart Ave. and washed up, my mother would have our supper on the table, which is now known as dinner. Later in the evening my father and I were back at the kitchen table for more lessons on carpentry. By then my home work was done and there was no such thing as television or running the streets, you were home preparing for the next day, Oh yes I was going to Cambridge Elementary School during the day but I was also home schooled at night.

Every now and then I would stop at the service station to see how my father was coming along with the building. If Max was there he would always strike up a conversation. He was very friendly and usually had a story or two to tell. Years later he had a home built on Alden Ave. diagonally across the street from our house, the builder was Ed Iwanicki. My father had retired a few years earlier and Ed told my brother that he knew my father was watching, so when it was time to shingle the roof he struck a number of choke lines all the way up the roof to make sure the shingles were perfectly straight from the top to the bottom.

Max and I became friends through the years. He was a good automobile mechanic. His wife Mary had a small appliance store on the left hand side of the building. She took care of all the paper work for the store and the service station, and oh' yes, she was a mother, a housewife, and a business partner. But let's not diminish the job that Max had to do. He was not just a mechanic he was the entertainer and salesman for this enterprise.

Now, let me give you an insight of the Max type hummer. In Philadelphia they had a radio station, WCAU, with a 50,000 watt transmitter and a tall antenna on top of the PSFS building. There was also a substation with another tall antenna in Moorestown, N.J. As kids, my brothers and I built crystal sets which received radio stations. The first station we received was WCAU loud and clear. There were always stories about this high powered transmitter, and here are a few. A man claimed he could hear WCAU while tying his shoe laces in the morning. An electrician said while performing tests in electrical boxes he could hear WCAU inside the box.

But here's the kicker; Max said, "Hey Harold did you hear the stories about WCAU?" My reply was, "Yes Max, I've heard a few". "Well listen to this! A guy came here yesterday to pick up his car, and claimed he was hearing WCAU every time he would grit his teeth". He worked for a grinding company and thought the grinding particles in his teeth were the problem. Max said he looked at the guy and didn't know whether to suggest a psychiatrist or a dentist. (Funny stuff I would say). This is the kind of humor you could expect from Max Berkowitz.

He was also a volunteer fireman just like most of us around town. Some were active and some were contributing members. Max was very active in his younger days. We had social events to raise money to keep the all volunteer fire company going. There were anniversary dinners and special fund raisers. At times, there were musicians among us, including myself, who would play music for certain parties. Hal Klingler played guitar, Del Thomson played accordion, Ray Jauss on banjo, and Max Berkowitz on violin. We certainly were young and the people enjoyed the music.

A few years later when Max and I were neighbors on Alden Ave., Bernie Berkowitz was about to get married. Max asked me if I could supply the music for Bernie's wedding reception at the house. I said, "Max! For you and your family the answer is yes." He thanked me and asked for one request; I said, "What's that Max?" He said, "Can you play Mazzletoff?" I said "yes, as long as you are going to sing." Just before the wedding I went over to his house with my guitar and he and I practiced playing and singing Mazzeltoff. I had more fun that day.

The day of the reception, John Smith, Harry Stevenson and I played songs that Max requested, and half way through Max got to sing Mazzeltoff. This was the highlight of his day. He was so proud of his son and daughter in-law that he could just about contain himself. After all these years, it's still quite memorable to me.

Their business, Berkshire's Super Service, was Max and Mary's lifetime enterprise. They had a moderate family of six: Peter, Bernie, Gig, Cyril, Irene and David.

Let me tell you about Pete Berkowitz. He is one of those people who go the last mile type of person. He was raised here in Riverside Park N.J. and I'm sure he's proud of that fact. He graduated from Palmyra High School in 1952 where he loved science and sports. Then he journeyed on to the state of Texas where he graduated from Southern Methodist University with a degree in chemistry. He then went to work for one of the large oil companies and traveled to the Far East to do research on oil samples. In later years he set his sights on a massive project to educate school children about the Holocaust and the more modern genocide that is going on in Sudan's western Darfur region. Pete would like the school children to choose right over wrong and good over evil. These lessons are good for a life-time, if they're taught at an early age. He also conducts tours for students to visit Houston's Holocaust Museum.

Pete Berkowitz is the chairman of the new Texas Holocaust and Genocide Commission and is now collecting and preserving Holocaust and genocide materials for future use in teaching school children in Texas and around his hometown of Houston about these atrocities. You just can't say enough about a person who will go that last mile for humanity.

Bernie also graduated from Palmyra High and like his brother Pete he played basketball and football all through high school. After graduation he pursued a job with PSE&G where, in time, became a supervisor. The rest of the siblings are doing fine. According to Bernie they were quite a bit younger than me, so I never had the opportunity to be close or get to know them.

Sam Zebrowski lived on Main St. in Cambridge with his wife, two daughter and three sons. He held a job at the Keystone Watch Case Co. He came to this country as a young man and dreamed of owning his own business. With the cooperation of his family, this was his start.

He was a big man and a gentle man with a good work ethic. In 1939 Sam called on my father to build a good size bar with a side room, where families could come for a meal and a drink. Back then it wasn't appropriate for women to go into a bar and drink with the men, so there were side rooms for the ladies.

The building was about 45 Feet long, with the left side for a bar and the right side dining room. The entrance was in the center of the building, with a large sign depicting the name. "The Park Inn." It was located on the corner of St. Mihiel Drive and Norman Ave.

There was a large room on the back of the building for a cooler and a kitchen. The door from the kitchen came into the bar and from there into the side room. The bar was pretty much the length of the room, with red leather cushioned seats and a brass rail to rest your feet on. The side room had a number of tables, each table sitting six, with white table cloths and low level contemporary music. It was relaxing.

Richard Zebrowski was the middle child, but quite a man and the drawing card of this establishment. He was tall, good looking, and had a pleasant manner about himself. He knew how to keep rule without dampening the fun and camaraderie that came with the territory. One of the topics, without question, would be the Garden State Park Race Track. Being only 20 minutes away, there was much enthusiasm about a certain breed of horses. How they ran in wet or dry weather, a fast or slow track, and many other depictions not to exclude the jockeys, the trainers, the owners and the stables they came from. The list goes on and on.

When you stepped up to the window to place a bet you had to be dam lucky, or really know what you were doing. Sometimes I think it's the thrill of seeing the horses coming down the stretch, heading for the wire, and you have a small wager win or lose. Richie seemed to have the best luck with horses. His brothers Ray & Al just couldn't keep up with him.

Ray and Al were in the asphalt business and weren't around too often. Al and I were in the boy scouts along with a lot of the kids around town. We all knew him as Bennie but his real name is Albin. His mother called him Binoch. The Polish mothers around town had special nick names for their sons. If the name was Edward, she would say Eddec and John was Yosshue.

Whenever the boy scouts had boxing matches the leaders would pick two boys and put these big 10 ounce gloves on them. After about a minute into the match your arms were so tired, you could hardly hold these gloves up. This one evening they matched me with Bennie. Bennie had about 20 pounds on me. Well I'm swinging away and my arms got tired. Bennie gave me a right to the side of my head and that was enough for me. I always said that Bennie Zebrowski gave me my first lesson in astronomy. I really saw stars that evening.

Richie Zebrowski and a part time bar tender, took care of the bar. One of the part timers was Francis Bart, who in later life seemed to have control over his drinking. He only worked four hours in the evening and then went home. I think he worked part time for his brother Ed Bart. In his younger days he had a few tricks to get a free drink at any bar. Every once in a while, when things were a little dull, Frannie would get up from the bar and say, "Who would like to hear Casey at the bat? Then someone would say, "If you can recite all of it, I'll buy the drinks".

Well you have to realize Casey at the bat has 13 verses, and all of them are about the same length. Here's the last verse. "Oh somewhere in this favored land the sun is shining bright; the band is playing somewhere, and somewhere hearts are light, and somewhere men are laughing, and somewhere children shout; but there is no joy in Mudville, mighty Casey has struck out." Not only would Frannie recite all 13 verses, he also used a good bit of theatrics, just as though he was standing at home plate, holding a bat, waiting for the pitcher to release the ball. Some people have a secret ambition to become an entertainer; it may have been one of Frannie's dreams.

Mrs. Zebrowski was a no nonsense woman. She was a mother that raised her children to respect everyone. You couldn't ask for a better family as they supported each other day after day. Raymond was the oldest, then Felicia and Richard, Sofia and Al. Felicia married and left home to work with her husband in their bakery shop business. This was a lifetime venture and they were very successful business people. Sofia and her mother did all the cooking and Sofia waited on tables in the side room. Even after she married, she still worked with the family. My mother, father, and my sister Eleanor and her husband, Eggy Horton and

I had many good meals there. You had to get there early Friday evening; the tables would fill up quick. Sofia was a good waitress and a beautiful and pleasant girl. If she had time, she'd sit at our table and chat with us. We always enjoyed her company.

There was a large lot on the opposed side of Norman Ave. In the summer, the fire company had a carnival that would come in and stay for a week. There was always a Ferris wheel, a carousel, games and side shows, apple taffy and cotton candy. It was a good fund raiser and people came out every night to enjoy the carnival and support the fire company. So many people ask me if I remember the carnival. How could I forget?

Around this same time Riverside Park had two teams that played ball on this good size piece of ground. The first was the Riverside Park Eagles football team, sponsored by Rapheal's Garage, with the help of Bill Gould, and the girl's softball team sponsored by Lydia Boenitsch's grocery store. These businesses helped us raise money for jackets and uniforms. Naturally, all games were suspended until the carnival left town.

On the far side of this lot was an unpaved road which is now Reserve Ave. There was one house at the very end, and I suspect it was once part of Hoffman's farm at an earlier date. The Bowker Family lived here for quite a few years. Elmer Anna-mae and two sons, Albert, Bobby, and a daughter, Larraine. Elmer and Annamae were the two nicest people you would want to meet. Elmer had a perpetual smile that was infectious, and you couldn't help liking this guy. He loved motorcycles and so did his two sons. As a master mechanic he knew every part and piece of his bikes. I think they were Harleys.

Elmer worked for Joe Reader who owned the property, all the way down to the Delaware River, and from Norman Ave to Dredge Harbor. He was contently dredging sand in this area for years. Elmer Bowker was in charge of all the machinery on land and on the dredger, and also the barges out on the water. He worked a good number of years for Joe Reader.

George Fields and his wife Irene and family lived on the right side of Reserve Ave., just in back of his brother Morrison on Norman

Ave. George was one of our service men who was a prisoner of war in Germany. When he came home he was 96 pounds of skin and bones. After a few months at home, his health improved to the point that he went back to driving trucks. Walt Malinowski, another prisoner of war, came home to Cambridge and weighed some 10 pounds less than George. Chick Bauer, who owned a dry cleaning business in Cambridge, was also a prisoner of war.

Later George continued to ride his Indian motorcycle and pickup girls and guys at the Dipsey Doodle and give them a ride of their life. He was one of those "Evil ken-evil" type guys and drove in stockcar races for the Anderson family. Yes, he was as tough as nails when need be, but in later life he became a dedicated father, husband, and gentleman the rest of his life.

Charlie Shinn had a few delivery trucks and started his business in Riverside, "Shinns Express". He also had a garage in Bridgeboro that burned to the ground. Then, in 1940, he purchased the property on St. Mihiel Dr. and Reserve Ave. This was the property of the National Lock Washer Co. They paid taxes up to 1940. Charlie wanted to expand his business, but before he could build, he had to remove a large portion of the old Lock Washer foundation. As school kids we would walk across the foundation on the way home from school. It was quite large, in fact it went back about 500 feet from St. Mihiel Dr., past the back yard of the Bowkers house, which is now part of Riverside Marina.

My grandfather, Gus Richter, worked for the National Lock Washer Co. as a Stationary Engineer. His work week started Sunday night at 11 o'clock. He would start the Corliss steam engine, with its 16 feet flywheel, which powered the rolling mills for the plant. At the end of the week he would shut the boiler down and the flywheel continue coasting for the weekend. This engine was setup in the back of the building, with the flywheel spinning toward the Delaware River in case it broke loose. If it spun in the opposite direction, it would have rolled through Cambridge. Charlie Shinn stayed here a short time, and then moved his trucking business to Stewart Ave. During his time in business he not only had Shinns Express, with some great looking trucks, he also had an extra axle added to one of his trucks for heavy hauling.

He also had a Bus Service that operated out of Riverside and transported passengers as far away as Moorestown, and also transported school students form Delran to Palmyra High School. This bus and "Kauderers" bus were the same make and model. We called this bus the Brown Bomber. The next house on St.Mihiel Dr. belonged to Louis Persic. The original house was a stone house when Lou purchased it. They lived there until the kids finished school and went off to college. Young Louie went to Cambridge school with us. He and I both went to Philadelphia for music lessons. He played accordion and I played guitar. We had many jam sessions at his house in the early days. In time, the old house was demolished and replaced with a beautiful brick mansion.

Lou Sr. came here as the captain of the American Dredging Company, which increased the size of Dredge Harbor. He also built the Castle Inn and the Castle Harbor Custard Stand. He was known as Captain Lou to his wife and friends. The "Castle Inn" was the first night club in this area and had a nautical theme that caught your attention as soon as you walked in the front entrance. The bar was built in a large square with room for the Bar Tenders, and a stage in the center which was elevated for the performers. The ceiling over the bar was concaved and housed a life boat with a set of oars.

Captain Lou Persic brought a lot of great talent from New Jersey and Philadelphia to the Castle Inn and it was one great place. Now I have to add a sad note. In the last few weeks Mary Persic at 103, and Rose Cosky at 102, have both passed away. They came here as young ladies from faraway lands, married and raised their families and stayed at their same homes on St. Mihiel Dr., Delran, Riverside Park, N.J., for a life time. God Bless them both.

Before these businesses were here it was mostly corn fields belonging to Lester Hoffman with one dirt road leading back to the Dredge. In the late 30's and early 40's this area of water was a lot smaller with a beach and a concession stand that had a dance floor and a jukebox at the rear of the building. It also had an outdoor movie. A cornfield with one dirt road and one foot path leading to St. Mihiel Dr., this area was known as the Dredge, it later became Dredge Harbor when the Parsons family started a marina over to the left side of this area.

A man by the name of Earl Chant operated the outdoor movie. There was a small area in back of the projection booth for cars, (naturally there weren't many cars back then), and in front there were long wooden benches to sit on and a large screen and a platform where John Smith and I played music at intermission time. I got acquainted with Earl Chant at that time and can say he ran a nice business. Everyone seemed to enjoy the movies.

During intermission there were lots of snacks and sodas at the concession stand, the jukebox was going full tilt with couples dancing the night away. My sister met her husband to be, Edward (Eggie) Horton at the dance. He enlisted in the Navy at the start of World War II. They had a short romance that lasted a lifetime. The war was upon us and the boys were leaving one by one. It kind of took the wind out of our sails but most of us survived, fortunately.

As Dredge Harbor Yacht built up their inventory of boats, there was part-time work available for us young guys. Ed Iwanicki was on first name bases with Bill and Herb Parsons and when Ed needed help he would call on his brother Ray and I. We would launch boats, wash them and pull them back on shore in the fall. I got to know Bill Parsons Sr. more than his brother Herb or their father who was also Herb. They were easy to get along with.

During 1944 the Crist Craft Boat Co. came to Dredge Harbor to promote their new company. They had been building small boats for the U.S. Navy all during the Second World War, and were trying to convince Bill Parsons into taking a Dealership for these new pleasure boats. Bill thought it wasn't the right time, for the fact that the war was still grinding on, and a lot of young men were still overseas. The salesmen from the company said that it wasn't common knowledge but the war was coming to a close, and by the time they got started the boys will be coming home and the Crist-Craft sales will be very good. He agreed to a dealership with Crist-Craft Co. That put Dredge Harbor Yacht on the map.

The Parsons have two children Bill Jr. and a daughter Tammie. They keep this business going in fine style. Their mother is still living in that beautiful 300 year old house which is a land mark and the oldest house in Delran. It was built by a farmer named Heulings, then sold to the Buck family, Washington Hunter bought it from the widow Buck. When you travel along St. Mihiel Dr .you'll notice a small bridge close to Dredge Harbor, this is Bucks Bridge. The house stayed in the hunter family name until the Parsons family purchased it.

Bill Parsons Sr. has passed, but he enjoyed 90 years of life, mostly here at Dredge Harbor Yacht Basin. I got to know Bill Parsons Jr. a chip off the old block; he is so much like his father. My daughter Cindy Klingler Wasco, Danny Cottrell, and Bill Parsons were at our house quite often, they graduated from Delran High in 1980. During their time at school they were active in the home coming activities and through the years Mr. & Mrs. Bill Parsons Sr. made room at the Dredge Harbor Yacht Basin for the decorating of the home coming floats. Ironically this is still the case today; the Parsons, Tammie and Bill, continuing the tradition as I write. They have a nice café' at dockside, if you've never been there try it sometime.

Moving on we come to the Monarch Boat Co. It was originally Monarch Building materials and hardware. The owner and operator was Edward Rutkowski, better known as "Monarch Eddie". When H.K. Porter purchased the Keystone Watch Case Co. there were only two Tool and Die makers left in the Tool Room, Ed. Rutkowski and I. We were having a conversation one night about how the Tool Making trade was slowly dying, that's when Eddie said he had put a bid on a piece of land and would soon go in business. That's all he would say and that was the end of the conversation. Eddie is long gone and the business which was Monarch Boat is also gone.

J&J Radiator is owned and operated by Joe Zeisweis and his son, Fran, Joe started the business in 1963. He came here earlier and got acquainted with a family of farmers by the name of Epollite. They owned large farms in Delran on both sides of Rt.130 from Millside Farms to Taylors Lane. One of the Epollite daughters married Fury Forcella who had a small auto repair shop not too far from Millside Farms. This is where Joe would get his car repaired. He was living in Philadelphia at the time working as a tool & die maker when he heard of a business for sale on River Rd. now St. Mihiel Dr, just this side of Taylors Lane. He jumped in feet first; This two bay garage with a small restaurant on one side was just what Joe was looking for. Soon he began to repair car radiators and that was the beginning of J&J Radiators still going strong today. His son, Fran, keeps the business going while Dad is semi retired. Many trucking companies send their radiators here to be repaired. It seems like no radiator is too big or too small, and I can say these two guys have the expertise in cooling systems. Their word and dependability is the hallmark of their success.

Jim's Flowers is another business that came along in 1969. Jim & Kathryn Hagan purchased this property from Lester Hoffman and then sold it to Jim & Linda Walter in 1974. They still sell flowers and the new name is The Harbor Deli where you can get breakfast and lunch. They do quite a business all year long. Stop in for breakfast or lunch, you'll enjoy it I'm sure.

The house next door belonged to Lester Hoffman, his wife Florence and two boys by adoption, Lester and Earl. In the late 30's and 40's he farmed all this ground from his house all the way down to Clarks Landing, I remember the corn fields here along River Rd. He also had a peach orchard in Cambridge in the area of where Lake Lonnie is today. In the back of his house he had a building and machinery for packing peaches.

There's one more house before McCarters Farm. This is where my friend Neal Wojceichowski and his sister, Bonnie grew up and attended Cambridge School along with my two brothers, Wayne and Francis. Neal spent time at our house with my brothers and their friends. Our backyard was 150 ft. deep, room for plenty of activities. Their mother was a home maker and their father worked at the Riverside Metal Co.

They were very good friends with Lester and Florence Hoffman and the McCarter's.

Eli Winford McCarter was born in Tennessee. Finished grade school with a scholarship to a Quakers Friend school in Tennessee. He endeared himself to the Quakers with his mild mannerisms and work ethic. They took him under their wing and when they migrated to the Cinnaminson area they brought Eli with them. This family by the name of Parry owned a good size parcel of farm land from the Delaware River out Taylor's Lane to the Burlington Pike (Rt. 130)

They sent Eli to the Quaker school of West Chester to finish out his schooling, when he graduated the Parry family had a job for him on the Taylor farm. Back in the early days this was all farmland and Eli was in his environment, he loved the rich soil and the cool summer breeze from the Delaware. Spring was like a second birthday that invigorated Wink, oh yes he had acquired this nick name "Wink" and it lasted for a life time.

He stayed in one of the small houses on Taylor's farm. After a few years working for the Taylor family he became like a son to the Taylors and he really felt like part of the family. His hard work paid off after a number of years, the Parry family who had taken an interest in Wink from the start, decided to give Wink a good size piece of farm land on the east side of the property along River Road which is now St. Mihiel Drive. Not only did he gain the gift of the ground, but the small house he was living in was moved to the farm facing River Road.

The house has been renovated and added to but still stands a few feet off of St. Mihiel Drive with a Farm Stand to the west side of the house. There were quite a few farms in the area, and one day Wink was smitten by one of the farmer's daughters. Everyone said they were a perfect match and Wink had a twinkle in his eye that was undeniable.

Well it wasn't long before the wedding bells were ringing and the two love birds married and settled down in this little farmhouse and raised a family of their own. Wink would farm this five plus acres of ground from spring through fall and as winter set in he would find work in the local foundries and metal companies in Florence and Riverside and Keekeffers cardboard box, in Pennsauken. N.J.

He worked for the Taylors all though the depression years, but now he was happily married and raising a family. The years were good to him and so he decided to open a farm stand to the Westside of the house. This little stand became a favorite place in the community for fresh fruit and vegetable. It's only known to a few of us that the original address of the McCarter farm was # 83 River Road, Riverside Park N.J. All of McCarter's farm, and property to the left, close to Taylors Lane and down to the Delaware River, then traveling east to the Rancocus Creek and culminating at Chester Avenue was the size of Riverside Park, N.J.

The McCarters' had one son Eli (Wink) McCarter Jr. and a daughter Joann McCarter (Dallman) who keeps this business going along with her husband and sons. This business has been here for a long time and serves the community as one of our anchor stores. If you've never been here, stop in, you'll enjoy that friendly atmosphere. "A little footnote" many times when I stopped to make a purchase, Eli would have a humorous story, not only funny but with a lesson for living. I love writing about these people from Riverside Park. Yes Eli's gone now and his last wishes where fulfilled, He was cremated and his ashes were sent back to Tennessee. "Well done Eli"… We miss you.

Part 9

Chester Ave.

Going down Chester Ave. toward the Rancocas Creek, the first house belonged to the Snow family. Unfortunately their father Joe Snow passed away at an early age from heart failure. This left Mrs. Snow with three sons and two daughters, Joe, John, Wayne, Darleen, and Phyllis to raise. This must have been a struggle for her to keep this house going and raise all these children, but somehow she managed to see them grow up, finish school, and go out on their own. I'm still amazed, I can't figure out how she did it.

The second house belonged to Joe Raphael and his wife Esmeralda. They had one son, Joe Jr., who had asthma, and lucky for him his mother was a registered nurse. Joe was told at the time, that his son Joey needed exercise to help his condition, so Joe had a pro tennis court built in the back yard. I know Joey tried playing the game of tennis, but sooner than later he became winded and went back in the house.

He seemed to get better after awhile. He and my sister Eleanor were in the same class. They graduated from Palmyra High School in 1941. They went to the World's Fair in New York City for their class trip. Then Joey went to college in Chicago, married and made his home there. He would continue writing to Eleanor for 60 years and she would write back, keeping him apprised of the latest happenings. You can leave your hometown physically, but in your mind it stays with you.

There were two or three rental houses, and then we come to the home of Joe Burk and his wife, two sons, John and Paul. John was the oldest. He was another builder in town and was mainly responsible for the building of the Riverside Masonic Hall on Chester Ave. Paul served in the US Navy during WWII, one of our Veterans that we were so proud of. You can see how people served their community and their country in so many ways. These are the kinds of people that blessed our neighborhood with the courage and fortitude to be there when needed.

At the corner lived the Pacevitch family, very reserved and hard working people. Pete worked for Rohm & Haas where they manufactured Plexiglas. If you've ever been in Bristle Pa. you'd know that sweet smell of Plexiglas that permeated the air, and everyone who worked there. That's why we called Pete Pacevitch the sweetest guy in town. He knew this little joke and was good hearted about it. Even after a shower and change of clothes, the people that worked there still had that sweet smell of Plexiglas about them, and let me make this clear, it wasn't unpleasant at all. Pete had a brother, Mike, who lived down the street. We'll get to him in due time.

Rather than cross the street, let's take a stroll over to Roland St. and then we'll come back on the other side. The first house is where we lived for a short while before moving to Stewart Ave. The second house belonged to Mr. & Mrs. Frank Warner. They had a daughter Beatrice who was an RN, and at times, she would patch up my cuts and bruises. Mrs. Warner sold the house when she was 90 years old and moved with her daughter, but before she moved she still cut her grass with a push lawn mower.

On the other side of the street there were two auto repair garages, operated by the McNulty family. Most of the cars they worked on were of the Ford variety like the model (T's) and model (A's). The McNulty's lived in the corner house of the second block on Chester Ave. John McNulty was also the Justice of the Peace for Riverside Park. He settled family disputes, traffic violations and disorderly conduct cases. For the most part he was very amicable.

Now continuing down Chester, the very next house belonged to Albert Malone, his wife and family. They had three daughters and one son. In order, there was Charlotte, Irma, Dolores, and Albert Jr. Irma and I were Classmates and lived around the corner from each other. Albert Jr. was a life guard at Holiday Lakes and Dredge Harbor. He was a very good one I must say, there were no drowning on his watch. There were quite a few drowning in the area due to the large amount of lakes, creeks, and harbors that fed from the Delaware River. Most of these drowning were caused by people falling off boats or children going near these waters unsupervised.

During the depression years Mr. Malone served as one of the many Relief Directors in the county. He was in charge of certain commodities, mainly food. Their house had small pieces of colored glass imbedded in the stucco, and around the flower beds were large pieces of colored glass. It was an eye catcher. South Jersey had a number of glass factories that turned out many types of glassware, and there was always a good amount of scrap glass to be purchased. Mr. Malone had a talent for landscaping with this glass and flower beds around his property and everyone admired his work.

I have to mention in passing that directly across the street from the Malone's on Chester Ave. and in Riverside, was the only house from St.Mihiel Dr., all the way down to the Rancocas Creek, save for one Boathouse at the foot of Chester Ave. The Daniels family lived there with their two sons who became electricians. Ironically both died at a young age from electrocution on the job. Sad to lose two sons this way but there weren't very good safety standards at that time. Their mother and father moved away and no one ever heard from them as far as I know. It was as though they disappeared from the face of the earth.

Now back to our side of the street. Edward (eggie) Horton and my sister Eleanor moved here at 25 Chester Ave. after the war. This was their first and last house. Eggie served in the US Navy during WWII. He was on the USS Melvin, a Destroyer that was in the battle of Leyte Gulf which included Iwo Jima and then sailed into Tokyo harbor and surprised the Japanese. The US Navy lost a few ships in the attack; they just wanted to send a message to Japan that they could be hit. This was one of the retaliation for the bombing of Pearl Harbor.

My sister was dating Eggie about a year before he got his draft notice. They liked to dance to the big band music. The hot spot around town was the Dredge Harbor Yacht Basin. They were married in 1942 while Eggie was home on leave. He went back for more training and in a few months he was home on leave for a short time, and then shipped out to sea. It wasn't too long before Eggie received a letter from my sister that he was about to become a father. His daughter Pamela was about two years old by the time he got home from the war. He received an honorable discharge and two Purple Hearts; another one of our heroes was home to stay.

They bought this house from Gus Volkman for $3,500.00 and paid it off in a short time. They added a son Eddie to the family and before we knew it both Pamela and Eddie were married and out of the house. Pamela had a son and a daughter and Eddie had two daughters, then tragedy struck. While his wife Doreen was driving across Rt. #130, another car ran the red light, striking her car broadside and causing her death.

Eddie moved back home with his two young daughters wondering what was next. It took some time for him to get over the death of his wife but in time he was out of the house, married and on his own. Eleanor not only raised these two granddaughters but also raised their sons and a daughter. Counting my mother there were five generations in the family. With all of this, you would wonder if anything else could happen in my sister's life. Well it did, but there was no sign how bad it would get.

Her husband, Eggie, was a happy guy, full of life and a joy to be around. Then the phone rang, it was my sister and she asks me to take Eggie to the doctors. My sister never had a driver's license and I lived one street away, she knew I'd be there in minutes. When I got there he was walking but dragging one leg. I got him in the car and took him to Doctor Metzer in Riverside. He sent him to the Veteran's Hospital in Philadelphia. Eggie made a few trips there but got no answer to his problem. He even got used to dragging this leg, but after time it become evident he had "Lou Gerigs disease".

As time went on he couldn't leave the house. He spent the last 6 years of his life at # 25 Chester Ave. in a hospital bed. My sister, Eleanor, would not let him go to a nursing home. She had a harness and a lift to get him out of bed and lower him into a chair. She washed him and fed him every day until he died. She also raised all those grandchildren at the same time. But wait, there's one more episode.

During the time she was taking care of Eggie and the grandchildren and great-grandchildren, she was diagnosed with lymphoma. She refused chemo therapy because of the responsibilities she had at home. She was a great cook and found a diet for this type of cancer, and with her determination she lived for 20 more years.

The next house belonged to Gus & Marge Volkman. They had a daughter and a son; in fact there were four or five families of Volkman's in town and we'll get to them in due time. Gus worked in one of the factories in Riverside. Marge was a home maker. Their son, Gus Jr., passed away in his early years due to a heart attack. Their daughter, Dorothy, married Gundie Jankowski, and Dorothy still lives in Delran. Dorothy and my sister Eleanor were very good friends over the years. Dorothy would visit Eleanor right up till the day Eleanor passed away. That's the type of friendship everyone needs. My thoughts and fond memories are still with my two sisters, Eleanore & Shirley.

Down a little further, a great piano player, Cecil Acton not only played but also tuned and repaired pianos; he also worked at the Keystone Watch Case Co. in Riverside. Cecil played piano in a lot of clubs and bars around town. John Steze established the White Eagle Bar on the corner of St. Mihiel Dr. and Chester Ave. It is quite a large building and half was dedicated for a dance floor, the other half for a rectangular bar, with a raised platform and a piano at one end. The bartenders had plenty of room around the platform to serve the patrons.

On both sides of the dance floor were tables and chairs and a small bandstand. Cecil Acton became the main attraction on Friday night. On Saturday night there would be a country western band, or a DJ, and lots of dancing. Cecil had a smooth way of playing contemporary music. He also wrote music and lyrics. I knew this from when we played music together. I still play one of the songs he wrote to his departed wife. Here is a sample of the words.

"Why can't we be together?"
"Why can't we have each other?"
"Dear you should know, I love you so"
"And what I've been saying is true."

The song goes on until it tugs at your heart strings. He remarried later in life and raised two daughters, Joan and Helen. Helen loved music and played drums, in fact they played together in some of the local clubs later in life.

Ted & Genevieve Steedle had two sons who became car salesmen. Not too long after they graduated from Palmyra High School in 1946-47, John landed a job working for Willard Dolby, who was a manager for the used car lot which was on St. Mihiel Dr. part way to Fairview St. Phil Crimmins had the dealership for Riverside Ford Sales on the corner of St.Mihiel Dr. and Stewart Ave., the former home of Raphael and Johnson's Garage, then became Canton Ford, and now the L&M bakery.

Dolby decided to leave Riverside Ford to work for Lucas Ford in Burlington. He was only there a short while, but before he left he recommended John Steedle as a car salesman, and Lucas hired him on the spot. It wasn't too long before John became "used car sales manager" for Lucas Ford. A year or so later Bill Steedle became a salesman for Lucas and as time went on, they both received awards as (Ford Five Hundred Club Salesman). They also received a plaque for the office wall, and a super bowl size ring with a diamond in the center and smaller diamonds around the sides for each year they were in the five hundred clubs, which was 15 years.

Bill married my sister, Shirley, and raised two daughters, Terrie and Donna. Once he became my brother-in-law, I never had to worry about buying a car. Whenever he saw the perfect low mileage car come on the lot, he'd call me that night and hold that car until I got there, which was the next day or two. I guess the deal was made from the time he called. Yes he had his repeat customers but most of his sales were Ford trucks.

Burlington County had its share of farms and Bill made sure these farmers got the truck they needed and on time. He sold more trucks to these farmers than any other salesman.

Another thing I'd like to point out about Bill, he never sold you a car; "you bought the car from him". There was no sales pitch, he knew what you wanted and when he met you at the agency he would talk sports right from the start. If he was talking about the Phillies, it was Cookie Rojas, his favorite baseball player. When Cookie came to Lucas Ford to promote some of Fords latest vehicles, he and Bill would talk about the Philly's management, players and new acquisitions Bill knew them all, and had his own opinion on the team as a whole. He became good friends with Cookie Rojas over the years. He sure had a lot of friends in upper management, not only with the Phillies but also with the Philadelphia Eagles, Buddy Ryan had his car serviced at Lucas Ford.

Here's a good story about car sales and meeting people. Bill, while making a sale to a football coach from the Philadelphia Eagles, just happened to mention Franko Harris from Mount Holly. The coach said, "Yes, I know him but he's too small." In the mean time Franko Harris went to Penn State and in a short time, he began his Pro Football career as the Pittsburgh Steelers' No. 1 pick and the 13th player selected in the 1972 NFL draft for 12 seasons. The 6 ft. 2 inches 230 pound from Penn State was a big yardage running back, a man in the powerful Pittsburgh Steelers' offensive machine. He was one of only four rookies in the NFL annals to rush for 1,000 yards. He was also on the receiving end of the "Immaculate Reception." The pass from Terry Bradshaw that gave the Pittsburgh Steelers their first ever playoff win, a 13-7 victory over the Oakland Raiders. In his 13 seasons, the last of which was spent with the Seattle Seahawks in 1984, Harris rushed 2,949 times for 12,120 yards and 91 touchdowns. Franko Harris was inducted into the Pro Football Hall of Fame in 1990.

Bill was so good with his customers that one person would recommend him to another. He was not only trusting, but a good guy with a great personality. One thing I almost forgot, Bill Steedle was an outstanding athlete and was nominated by Robert Heck and inducted into the Palmyra High School Sports Hall of Fame in 1946. Bill's senior year, he lettered in four sports (Football, Basketball, Track and Baseball.) When Bill retired from Lucas Ford, I bought all my cars from John Steedle. John was the General Manager at Lucas Ford and he treated me with the same courtesy as brother Bill did.

Bill was drafted into the US Army during the Korean War, and served his entire time in Okinawa. Whenever they had time to spare, Bill would form a baseball team to keep the men's sanity. For one reason or another, Bill always became the home plate umpire, coach or catcher and again, I have to say that Bill was one of a kind, an outstanding athlete.

John also loved sports but lost a kidney playing football with the Riverside Park Eagles. He still lives in Delran and is now retired from Lucas Ford. He is an avid fisherman with a house on Long Beach Island where he always owned a fishing boat. John and I keep in touch, and even though time keeps slipping away, our friendship goes on and on. They raised a son, John, and a daughter, Dawn, who addressed us as Aunt Elaine and Uncle Harold. These are the things that stay with you for a long time. One note, John's great-great uncle Morris Steedle served on the first Township Committee of Delran in 1880.

A little further down lived Harry Klemm & his wife Marie. He worked as a mason mostly installing sidewalks and foundations for homes. They had one son Herman who attended Cambridge Elementary School and then went on to Palmyra High School where he played football and track. I can remember being at their home on Chester Ave., and I guess Hermie being an only child could get away with a lot more than we ever thought of. His mother, Marie, would move the dining room table over to one side of the room so the boys could play touch football. The doorways between the living room, dining room and the kitchen were in line and it wasn't unusual to see Hermie throw a pass from the living room to Jack Esworthy, who was in the kitchen. Bill Steedle and Marvin Heck were trying to intercept the pass while Marie would stand by just to keep some sort of order, but you could see she enjoyed every moment of this inside football game.

Hermie had a pet turkey that wandered around the yard. I think the turkey name was Franklin. But to get to the heart of this story, Franklin had a fascination with a female turkey named Betsy. She resided at the Millside Farms residence which was at the end of Chester Ave. and Rt. 130. At certain times Betsy would give out a love call and Franklin's head would dart up and before anyone knew it Franklin would be in flight. It wouldn't be long before Mr.Lashlockey who owned Millside farms would be on the phone asking Hermie to kindly come and get Franklin. I can't remember what happened to Franklin, he just seemed to disappear one cold day in November,"yumee".

After graduating from Palmyra HS in 1946 five of the Riverside Park boys Hermie Klemm, Bill Steedle, Marvin Heck, Whitty Bembow and Frank Breuer decided to join the Blair AC football team of Riverside. They played a couple of seasons to fill in the gaps for a shortage of men, due to the Second World War. The men coming home were so "War Weary" that they needed time to get their lives together.

Then we had a recession that lasted into the 1950's, and then the Korean War came along and Hermie was drafted into the U.S. Army. At the time, we had service men in many parts of the world. When you were drafted you could be sent to Germany, Korea or Japan. When some of the boys received their notice, they immediately signed up with the Navy or Marines.

Herman was sent to Germany and that's where he served his time. The Army took these boys and turned them into men in a very short time, and believe me, I was one of them. I'm sure you noticed that Hermie is now Herman. There were no nick names in the service except with your buddies. Herman came home in 1953 after serving his time in the Army. He married his one and only sweetheart Dolores, who later gave him two beautiful daughters.

It didn't seem long before tragedy struck...Herman suddenly became ill in 1955. After a number of tests, he was diagnosed with cancer. He was sent to John Hopkins Hospital for some experimental treatments. I'm talking about cancer back in 1955 when not much was known about it and the word alone was a certain death sentence. Herman and the family were clinging to the only hope they had, and continued with 8 years of treatment but to no avail. He passed away Aug.15, 1965, and he had all the attributes of an "all American boy". What a waste, what a shame.

I can't remember who lived in the next house but after WWII Gert Lipinsky married Ray Iwanicki and they purchased this house next to her sister, Margaret Toffle. They had one daughter, Linda, and soon became members and trustees of the Park Community Church. Life seemed good to them for a number of years but then Ray suddenly became ill. He spent time in and out of the hospital but his heart gave way and we lost him forever; but I must say, Ray and I had a lot of good times together. "Amen brother Ray".

At the end of the block lived the Toffle family, Fredrick and his wife Margaret (nee) Lipinsky and a son Bill who worked in communications as a radio announcer in Philadelphia, Pa. and also a daughter Grace. They were very reserved and nice people to have as neighbors. Margaret was the oldest of the Lipinsky family from Alden Ave. Fritz, as we knew him, was a lifelong member of the Riverside Turners, and helped with the building and the organization which promoted good health and physical fitness. He was like so many other emigrants who came to this country, and was eager to help build strong communities.

The side street between Chester & Stewart is Fredrick St. The Beddel family Roland & Betty lived here and raised two daughters. The only other house on this side of the street belonged to Lou Bauer's. There were only corner houses on the other side of Fredrick St., Roland Beddel had tinkered with automatic transmissions when they first came on the market and only a few car makers were using them. After graduating from Palmyra HS he decided to go into business and opened up a transmission repair shop. It wasn't long before he became well known around this area as a highly qualified transmission mechanic. Most of the auto shops sent their cars to him and he was the fore runner in automotive transmission repair in this area.

Lou and Marion Bauer lived in this other house on Fredrick St. Lou worked for the Pennsylvania Rail Road where he lost one leg working as a Brakemen. They had a daughter Marion, who married Chas Atkinson, they bought a lot on Stewart Ave., and Chas built a beautiful brick home next to what is now known as Friendship Park. Chas was a charter member of the Delran Emergency Squad.

Rhoda Wells lived at the corner of Fredrick & Chester, Ave. There were only about 65 houses in this little town and empty lots between homes. There were two lots between Rhoda's house and the Fox family house. In time there were houses built on both of these lots.

Toward the end of the Great Depression the Fox family came upon a stroke of bad luck, and their mother, Florence, suddenly had this small home and five children to take care of. You can hardly imagine the anguish she was suffering at the time but she pulled herself together with one thought in mind; all the decisions were hers to make from now on. It wasn't easy to keep a family together. Jobs were still hard to come by but she was determined to be the bread winner, if not, the state would step in and the children would be gone.

She found small jobs in the beginning but the two jobs that sustained her family for most of the years were the Toy Factory in Burlington and Century Mills in Riverside. She had three sons and two daughters. The oldest son, Edward, was 10 years old at the time his father left and in six years, at the age of sixteen, he quit school and went to work to help his mother support the family. He never complained as he thought it was his duty to do whatever possible to make things right, not only for his sisters and brothers but, for his mother whom he loved dearly.

Ed is a very soft spoken man and when I interviewed him just a few months ago he admitted quitting school just to help support the family. We've been friends for a lot of years and shared old stories with each other. The one we liked the best was when his brother, Kenney, and my brother, Wayne, were mixed up at the Zurbrugg Hospital in Riverside. It was lucky that both mothers were in the same room when they were to leave. The nurse had mixed up the babies and before my mother and Ed's mother left they questioned the nurse. I guess you call it mother's intuition. There was a mix up and it was all straightened out. Years later we talked about the mix up and how the two boys had looked similar in their younger days.

Ed's wife, Charlotte (nee) Bozarth was also from the Park. Her mother and father and one sister lived on Chester Ave. for a short time. Later they moved to a house on River Drive between Stewart and Alden Ave. I met her mother briefly while at the house. Charlie and I struck up a friendship through music. He played guitar, accordion and piano, and I played guitar and accordion. It may seem ironic but Charlie Bozarth had two brothers, Russell and Atwood, and they all played music. Russell played banjo and Atwood played alto saxophone. Not only that, but as machinists, the four of us worked in my uncle Paul's machine shop on Stewart Ave. These three boys were talented, as they also had a good amount of knowledge in carpentry work. I sure had the pleasure of visiting each one of them in their homes at different times.

A few years ago Ed came to my house for guitar lessons, and Charlotte would come with him. After a while I noticed she knew quite a bit about music theory and like her father she played piano. I guess that shouldn't have been a surprise to me.

Pete Pacevitch's brother, Mike, got married and moved down into the last block of Chester Ave. He loved masonry work and you can still see the pillars in front of the house with small pebbles placed in the cement surfaces. This was a project and I guess his hobby because he worked on it for years.

George Murphy was a Machinist and worked at the Riverside Metal Works. He was a very soft spoken man and a delight to know. He married one of the Shedecker girls from Riverside and raised three daughters here in the Park. After the girls finished high school they married and moved out of town. Like so many families, once the children leave the nest and are on their own, there is no need for a large house and so the parents move on. In some cases we never see them again.

Charlie Schwartz lived down close to the Rancocas Creek. He moved here after he left the navy. He was a good musician. In fact he played the saxophone for John Philip Sousa in the US Navy band. He gave music lessons here in town and at his home. Charlie never owned a car. He would hop on his bicycle with his music book and clarinet in the basket, and peddle to a student's home, give the lesson, then be off to the next home. He also scheduled his meals in between and gave lessons at his home in the evening.

I remember getting my first accordion lessons from Charlie. He had hand written music notations by John Philip Sousa. It was quite a collection. When Charlie taught he used the Sousa method which stated that all music has notes and punctuations just like a sentence. Charlie taught this to all his students.

Here is the sentence, with and without punctuation.

(That that is, is; that that is not, is not; is not that it? it is! that that is not.)

(That that is is that that is not is not is not that it it is that that is not)

Charlie never married. He lived in the same house and earned a living with music until the day he died.

Fred and Bessie Pfeffer lived at 85 Chester Avenue, the last house at the end of the street. Fred worked at the Town Luggage Company in Riverside. They had three sons and a daughter. During the Second World War Fred's brother George was drafted into the U.S. Army. Before leaving he put his cream puff 1938 Chevy in the garage, greased most of the metal parts, waxed the body and covered it with canvas. When he returned home after the war his brother Fred rented him a room while he built his own house on Stewart Avenue. They were both musicians. George played accordion and Fred played clarinet and saxophone. Most of the musicians around town admired Fred and his musicianship. He could make a clarinet talk.

I remember being at the Turners Hall for a wedding reception where Fred and his group were playing. Someone requested the clarinet polka and as a musician I can tell you, this is a master piece for the clarinet. Fred got a standing ovation when he finished. Fred was one of those rare musicians that had to practice every day for at least an hour or two. There was another musician that had this stick to it attitude and you may know him, a great guitarist Al Lacony. There may have been others but these two were my close friends.

Over the years I became friends with Fred & Bessie's children. The oldest were twins, (Fred & George), then Janice, then Bill, who wanted to do everything under the sun just to try and keep up with his older twin brothers. He was tall skinny and all arms and legs, not knowing what to get into next.

Here are "excerpts" of an interview I had with Bill and some of his writings. (Quote) At the early age of five I began to grow up fast in "The Park" and learning the ways of the boys in the neighborhood that were friends with my older brothers. Here are the names I remember ....

Jimmy and Johnny Eigenbrood, Mel Hess, Gene Karachewski, Bill Toffel Bobby Volkman, Bobby & Bert Bowker, Fred & Bobby Becker, just to name a few. Although I had my own friends, that is, Jimmy Maher, Joey Eigenbrood, Keith Locker, Ed. Horton, Teddy Karachewski, Bobby Woodington, Joe & Roy Bowker; but somehow I would find myself getting involved with the older guys, especially my brothers' friends."

Bill said that his father kept a row boat at the end of Chester Ave. in the Rancocas Creek. A chain and cinderblock with a lock kept the boat near the water's edge. Well, one day Fred and George decided to take the rowboat out as usual and he, Brother Bill, decided to tag along for the ride. Little did he know that when they reached the opposite side of the creek he would be thrown overboard and told to swim back home. They knew he could swim and also knew that they would be close by, just in case. Well by the time he made it back he was 300 to 400 yds downstream. I and a lot of others who have tackled the Rancocas Creek, in one way or another, know how swift the tide runs at certain times of the day. You really have to know the water ways when boating or swimming.

Bill also talked about the early days when we had milk and bread truck delivery. The milk came from Millside Farm's and the bread came from Freihoffers Bakery. He said that one of their favorite tricks was to remove the note that his dad had stuffed in the empty milk bottle for Freihoffers Bakery and wrote a new note with doughnuts and cakes added to their dad's list. "Boy did we ever pay for that."

As kids we played every imaginable "make up game" you could think of. From "kick the can" to "name that tune" to "I spy." We didn't have computers, walkman, or I-pods etc. But we had a good time down here in the "Park". The Pfeffer boys also talked about the opposite side of Chester Ave. which is Riverside Township. It was nothing but a wooded area with dirt roads going over to "swampoodle". This was part of the old Stewart farm. Somewhere in the 1920's there was one barn that the Township demolished. It sat on a large hill and was great for sledding in the winter.

In the mid 50's a builder named Fucco bought up approximently 50 acres of this land and began building a residential neighborhoods of about 400 homes. The Pfeffer's and a few of the other boys would play hide and seek after the workers went home for the day. About twice a week the kids would collect the empty soda bottles that the workers left and cash them in at Boenitsch's store up on the main street. "Bill said he would not give up his childhood for anything. It was one adventure after another, day after day".

Bill loved sports and Fred & George would tutor him in his pursuit to become a decent baseball player. Then in 1956/1957 word had it that a Little League team was going to be organized for the Riverside Park / Cambridge kids. The field was going to be staked out and bulldozed right where Mac Millian's, (now Simon & Schuster) is situated in the Cambridge section previously Kentzingers' farm. Bill said it was exciting watching the bulldozer leveling the ground at this site which would soon become the first Little League Field this side of Rt. 130.

It wasn't long before invitations were announced for tryouts. "Mr. & Mrs. Verner, of Leon Ave., Cambridge, were to be our first of many coaches along the way". Their son Joe was an excellent ballplayer also. Bill said that his brothers, Fred and George, had drilled him for years to become a pitcher, and by the time the Little League Team was ready to go, he was ready, or so he thought. The field was very rough by today's standards. Thousands of small stones were gradually removed by the players and the rickety picket fence needed daily mending, but like Bill Pfeffer said enthusiastically, "The Park & Cambridge boys finally had their ball field and ball team."

During the first season they had to play the likes of "St. Petes Keys",

Delanco, and a couple of other teams. Bill started out as a pitcher. He could throw the ball right down the heart of the plate every time. That's what got him in trouble. Bill said that the teams they were playing were organized for some time and also had a few older boys playing. He remembers getting beat 42 to 2 and 38 to 1, it was terrible. But finally, one day when they were getting pounded, our catcher, Ritchie Janzewski, called time out. As we gathered at the pitcher's mound with the coaches, Ritchie suggested to Mr. Verner that if there could be a change in positions with him; Ritchie, pitching and Bill Pfeffer catching. Coach Verner gave the ok and from that day forward they never looked back. This move was the beginning of many, many championship teams over a period of years. "From Little League up to Babe Ruth, it seemed like no one could beat us and Ritchie was one huge reason why! Boy could he pitch and he could also hit". He went on to be drafted by the Atlanta Braves; however it was not to be. During this era, there team piled up championship after championship.

These are some of the coaches starting with Mr. Verner. Then there was Bob Engle, Bill DeNight, Joe Chinicci, Tony Marcelli, and Walt Yansick.

The other prominent figure were Charles Molitor, Tom Johnson, Walt Yansick Jr., Phillip Massey, Bill Goodheart, Andy Latanzzi, Kevin Gross, and Coach Tony Marcelli. These were the very first "Traveling Teams" Delran AA had organized. They were entered in the Delaware Valley "Pony League" and they won championships both years while my friend Bill Pfeffer was a member of the team.

Following the second season with the traveling team, Bill said, "We were old enough to play with the big boys", (Babe Ruth Traveling Team). We played the likes of Moorestown, Cinnaminson, Merchantville, Riverside, Delanco, Lenola, Rancocas Woods, Sacred Heart of Palmyra, and others. Here are some of the player's names. Horace Crider, Don Hamlin, Howard Rendfry, Rich Janzewski, Bill Zube, Bill Avery, and yours truly Bill Pfeffer. "We won championship after championship; every team was gunning for us. Some even consolidated with each other, putting their very best out on the field, but to no avail, we were simply that good and talented".

Bill's twin brothers, Fred & George, more or less speak as one. They told me that two more houses have been built between their childhood house #85 and the Creek. When I interviewed Fred, this is what he had to say. (Quote) "I grew up with my twin brother George, sister Janice, and brother Bill. George and I were the oldest, born on February 3rd, 1941. My sister Janice still lives at that address, with her husband Fred Neuman. Fred was a classmate of mine in the class of "59", Riverside High School. My brother Bill is six years younger than George and I. We still live within four blocks of each other. Yes, my father was a fine musician and we all remember how he practiced. He was a real pro. When we were young my mom, Bessie, worked at the old original Grants in Riverside, WOW! What a wonderful time to grow up in "The Park."

Fred & George made friends easily; they were the best of the best and a product of a mother and a father who knew how to raise children. Sometimes I'm over whelmed when I think and write of the good people here in "The Park." These two twins were always together, and at a young age they made friends with the Nauss brothers, Jack & Don, who lived at the end of Stewart Ave. Fred talked about their first encounter with these two rascals. Fred & George were blessed with big ears but never thought much about it. Well, one day they decided to check out the Nauss's house which was the last house on Stewart Ave. facing the creek. As they crossed the street out came Jack & Donald running after them with penknives, shouting "We're going to cut your ears off!" Well, you can imagine how scared they were but then they realized it was just a joke and the four boys became life-time friends. Mr. and Mrs. Nauss were great people with a large hard working family. Fred talks about how Mr. Nauss would let them in the yard to pick pears from his pear tree which they carted home for their grandmother who would stew them and put them in jars.

Here's another (Quote) from Fred. "I remember one day shortly after becoming a police officer for Delran, and while I was sitting in my patrol car in the driveway of the motel at Chester Ave. and Route 130, and Mr. Nauss saw me and pulled in. He gave me some nice words of encouragement that I never forgot". There was also a pier at the end of

Stewart Ave. and a gold colored seaplane that would practice takeoffs and landings at Plum Point. They could take off and fly right past Stewart Ave. It was actually a bright yellow J2 Piper Cub with pontoons. Fred said that he and George would shout to this plane, "Come get us, take us for a ride" in fact I've witnessed five or six kids shouting at the top of their lungs "take us for a ride."

Well they finally realized that these young men were flying with an instructor, learning how to take off and land.

Here's Fred again. (Quote) "George, myself, and for that matter, my sister Janice and brother Bill grew up attending the Park Community Church and Sunday School. For many years we would have perfect attendance. A lot of times we didn't want to go, but my dad would take off his belt and say, "Which do you want!" And so off to Sunday school we went. For that, I will be eternally grateful. I believe Mr. and Mrs. Hunsinger started this church. Some of my teachers were Florence Albright, John Emrick, Walter Young, Joe Harris, (who could scare the hell out of you), and Bill Lipinsky. By the time we were twelve or so we had a pretty good grasp of the bible from cover to cover. I've always admired all of those wonderful teachers. I believe that what they did for us will vibrate through eternity. At the age of thirteen, George and I led in prayer with Pastor Ron Holtz and accepted Jesus Christ as our Lord and Savior. As I look back on my seventy one years, and I can say without a doubt; surely goodness and mercy has followed me all the days of my life.

Part 10

River Drive

River Drive is the road that runs along the Rancocas creek. Along these banks were three boathouses which were established long before the town. There were pilings driven in the bank and out in the water. The houses were built on pilings from the bank all the way out in the water and their fishing boats were tied to a dock that extended out from the back of the boathouse. They were fisherman by trade and made a living by catching fish and taking them to Philadelphia markets across the Delaware River.

This area is the beginning of the Rancocas Creek, which feeds off of the Delaware River. These boathouses were here at this particular place and could view Philadelphia markets across the Delaware River. As the families passed on the property became abandoned and the township had them demolished. In fact, these properties were never titled. The last boathouse at the end of Chester Ave. was torn down in 1958; there were a few boathouses across the Rancocas creek that was somewhat the same. **Fred Wolff** made a painting of that old Boathouse.

On the south side of the street between Chester and Stewart, was the Marshall family home which has been torn down. They had six daughters, Evelyn, Mildred, Doris, Jackie, Edith, and Lois. Two of the girls married and stayed in "The Park" their whole life. Edith married Ed Iwanicki and Mildred married Jimmy Maher. (I'll tell you about my friend Jimmy later).

I have to mention our public works employees. Especially Larry Jack who was one of the best Supervisors of Public Works we've had, and the men who worked with him such as Jack Horner, Bud Smith, Ron Jankowski, Arthur Coleman, Ben Salkowski, Larry Urwiler, Joe Swadgeus, Bob Gavin, Kevin Sarlo. These are the people we depend upon when the snow is up to our hips, or the leaves are clogging our streets. Sometimes when the Rancocas Creek is working its way up the streets, we never know when we may need them. These men and many more have always been here rain or shine.

The Dipsey Doodle with Edith Marshall and Albert Pipit.

Canton Ford, Now L&M Bakery

My Grandmother and Grandfather's House

My Grandfather's car accident.

Dredge Harbor Boat Center

National Lockwasher Steam Engine with 16 foot fly wheel

J&J Radiator

McCarter & Dallman Flowers

The Park & Cambridge Boys Little League

Fred Wolff's Painting of The Boathouse

Howard Wills 46 ft. Cabin Cruiser, The Seagull

The Klingler Machine Shop

Delran's Flag and Seal Designed by Fred Wolff Sr.

The Stone House, originally part of the Stewart Est.

The Stewart Family farm house

The Swedes Run Fork found by Wayne Klingler

Part 11

Stewart Ave.

In back of the L&M Bakery there's a parking lot where once stood another mom & pop store owned and operated by the Bart family. Next to that, was the Bart family home. The family had a tragic accident at this house in 1930. Very few cellars had concrete floors and Bart's had a dirt floor. They had contracted sand flees on their cellar floor. The remedy was to spray with some type of insecticide, but in this case, Tom Bart decided to use gasoline. The irony of this tragedy was the fact that in the cellar there was an electric water pump to supply water throughout the house. I remember this type of water system. When you turned the faucet on the electric motor would start and pump water as you needed it. If a faucet was dripping, in time, the low pressure would cause the pump to start. These electric motors had brushes that made sparks.

Now, with the cellar filled with gasoline fumes, what happened next you can well imagine. A spark from the pump ignited the gasoline fumes and the explosion lifted the house off of its foundation. Men from the garage next door rescued the three victims from the house, sending them to the local hospital. Tom and his son Mathew, never survived their injuries. Mrs. Bart and her son Francis were working at the store that day, they were very lucky. Young Eddie remembered himself and the couch he was laying on, having been lifted up to the ceiling and then crashing back down to the floor. He only suffered minor cuts and bruises. The house was put back on it foundation and is still there today,

Mrs. Bart continued to operate the family store with the help of her two sons. Her youngest son, Eddie, stayed around the home and the store. On occasion he went to Dock Street in Philadelphia early in the morning with his brother, Francis, to buy produce for the store and the huckster wagon which his brother, Francis, drove around town. The huckster truck or wagon had open sides and back with a canvas top. Each side had stair step shelving to show off the fruits and vegetables. In the back would be small sacks of potatoes.

While we're on the subject of huckster wagons, you may remember in the 1930's there were wagons and trucks going through the neighborhood, buying or selling one thing or another. Some would buy rags and some would buy metal. Each had a scale and would pay by the pound. There were men who sharpened knives and scissors and others who repaired umbrellas. There were also milk deliveries from Millside Farms.

In the meantime, Francis got married and moved up the street Eddie and his mother lived in back of the store and kept the business going, Francis Bart was a good huckster, everyone liked him. I myself had sympathy for this friend of mine for he suffered from alcoholism; probably it was the result of the family tragedy. Yet, he was still the proverbial happy go lucky town alcoholic.

Let me see if I can convey a sense of righteousness about this man. He must have taken after his mother. She was another big hearted woman who knew the needs of the community. Many times, being in the store, I would look at her with such admiration. She had a way of greeting you with this pleasant look that was infectious. As a young kid her demeanor fascinated me. More than once, if four of us were in the store for ice cream and there was just enough money for three, while on our way out you could almost bet that the last straggler would be called back by name. And, as he or she turned back, Mrs. Bart would be holding out another cone, probably with just the right flavor of ice cream. I know Francis had his mother's genes for he had a big heart and never a cross word for anyone.

Later, as a young man, Eddie Bart married Dorothy Siegfried. They moved into the Bart house that I speak of. They started a business; Bart's

Flowers Inc., and then moved the business to Creek Road in Delran, N.J. They have a daughter, Sandra, and a son, Tom, 7 grandchildren and 3 great grandchildren. Ed is gone now but Tom and his son run the business with the help of Dorothy as the bookkeeper. It must have been traumatizing for Eddie losing his father and brother, Mathew, at that young age, however he would never let you know. He went on with his life and always greeted you with a smile.

Lester and Elva Grob live here on Stewart Ave. with their son and daughter. Lester inherited this property from his father which had a large piece of ground in back of the house. His father, John, worked for PSE&G and I would have thought that Lester would follow in his father's footsteps like a lot of the young boys did at the time. But Lester wanted no part of it even though PSE&G was a great company to work for. Lester decided to go into business for himself. It wasn't long before a building was going up on that piece of ground in back of the house, and soon Lester opened up a Tailor Shop where he did cleaning pressing and alterations. The people around this area liked his work and the fact that he hired full time and part time workers from here in the Park.

Harry Miller, his wife, Frances, and daughter, Shirley, moved into the Bart house. Harry and Frances dedicated a lot of their time to the local fire company, he as a fireman and her in the ladies Auxiliary. Quite a lot of wives and daughters belonged to the Auxiliary and were always there to cook for annual dinners and social events, raising money for the fire company. Harry was a bartender by trade, "and quite a good one". Back in the 40's a good bartender was an asset to the business. They were the drawing card so to speak. Harry was a robust kind of a guy, full of life, and from behind the bar had an anecdote for most situations. "You came into the bar with a tear in your eye, and left with a smile on your face". "That was Harrys Forte".

Across the street was a large lot and a double house belonging to the Iwanicki family. They had two daughters and three sons. The father and mother were emigrants who came from Poland to Ellis Island and then to Riverside Park where they made their home. Stanley worked in Philadelphia for the Bud Co. He rode the public service bus as many others did. One day Stanley got off the bus with a cast iron hot water radiator. It was 30 inches high and two feet long and very heavy. His son, Ed, went up the street with a wheel barrel and brought the radiator home. Back then people would be standing in the aisles of the bus, holding on to a Christmas tree. They didn't have cars like today so this was the mode of transportation and the bus company tried to keep the people happy. When someone would be in the back of the bus, and had to get off at the next stop, they would pull on the cord and the bus would slow down as this person worked their way through the Christmas trees to get off the bus.

Ed Iwanicki was the last one left living at the family home and I think he was born there. His sister, Bertha, and her husband, Toby Mosteller, lived in the other half for a few years. When the Korean War came along Toby enlisted in the Marine Corp and was lucky to come back in one piece. Ed served in the US Air force, WWII, as an engineer on a B24 bomber. All of the crew was college graduates except Ed; he was right out of high school when Uncle Sam called. He told me of the many bombing raids he made on the Japanese islands. They would fly in low close to the water, and as they came to the trees, they would drop their bombs. The squadron kept this going week after week and you can imagine the tree line moved back and the shore line became larger. Consequently the Japanese had to keep on the move, and at night, he said they would fly dummy raids to keep the enemy from sleeping. Each crew had to fly (40) forty bombing missions, then a new squadron would take over.

When Ed finished his 40 missions the new squadron was one engineer short. The captain went into one of the barracks and asked for a volunteer. A hand went up. The captain said, "What is your name sergeant?" "Ed Iwanicki sir". The captain said, "thank you, I know you'll be an asset to squadron (B). Make sure you report to Lieutenant Smith in the morning." During the war these fly boys were lucky to survive (40) missions and were happy when they finished. Having volunteered for one more mission was an act of bravery. Well, he came back safe and sound with (41) missions, a true American Hero in every sense of the word.

When he came home he became a builder. He built and remodeled private homes and he was also a good mechanic. He could completely rebuild an automobile engine and even convert it into a marine engine. He loved fishing and always had a boat. His brother, Ray, was in the US Navy and also in the Pacific during the war. One day Ed received a letter from Ray, and here they were both on the same island. Ed went to the Captain and received permission to hop in a jeep with a driver and visit his brother Ray. How often have two brothers from the same town met on a little island in the Pacific.

Living in the other half of this house was Gus Seigfried, his wife, and two daughters, Helen, Dorothy, and a son we knew as Gusie or Junior, named after his father. He was a good boy who suffered from epilepsy and when he had a seizure, we as boys of the neighborhood, would comfort him until the seizure was over. Later on, we were saddened when Gusie lost his life going across the tracks at Chester Ave, crossing. I think there were only flashing lights back then; no gates at this particular crossing. Gusie had a habit of walking with his head down. He may have noticed that when looking straight ahead for a period of time it could bring on a seizure. But this is only speculation as his family seemed to think this was one of his problems. There were a few who lost their lives on those tracks between Riverton and Riverside.

We moved from Roland St. to #10 Stewart Ave. while my father built our new home on Alden Ave. While we lived here, a neighbor, Mrs. Kessler, gave me harmonica lessons and I was also taking accordion lessons from Charlie Schwartz. One day I went up to Bart's store and met up with the Iwanicki brothers, Ed, the oldest, and Ray, about my age. They lived across from the Bart's store and after making a few trips to the store, Ray and I become friends. Ed was the enforcer on the street and made that evident from the start. I found this out the day I walked out of Bart's store with a penny's worth of candy and bumped into Ed. He immediately demanded half of what I had and I knew I had no alternative but to comply. When he got his half he stepped aside and I went on my way.

Most of the guys around town addressed him with the nick name "halfy". He always wanted half of everything. Later on I earned the privilege of calling him Ed. But whenever I made a wrong turn he would take me to task until I agreed with his way of thinking. No one came down Stewart Ave. without Ed's approval. His brother, Ray, and I together, didn't weigh as much as he did. He was a big and strong "pa'pol'ski" with an iron fist. There's one thing I can say and that is, no one could lay a hand on Ray or me without answering to Ed. I don't want to leave the impression that Ed was a bully, he was just acting as a disciplinarian, and I, being a few years younger hadn't quite caught up with the rules of the road. Yes there was a difference between us. I attending Cambridge Public School, and Ed, attending St. Casmir's Parochial School. For awhile I thought he was the Monsignor.

We became very close, like three musketeers that is, including Ray, who was like a silent partner while Brother Ed was around. We would travel around the river banks to see what we could find. On days after a hard rain we would tramp over to Cambridge woods to look for Indian arrow heads. We had a fair collection but don't ask what ever happened to them.

Ed was an inquisitive type person and sometimes got himself in trouble. An example of this was the time when in a chemistry class, the teacher placed water and a cork in a test tube then held it over a flame until the water changed to steam and the cork flew out and hit the ceiling. Immediately after school Ed was in the back yard with a one gallon glass jug and a small amount of water with a cork in the top. He then proceeded to build a fire and when he held the glass jug over the fire he told us to stand back and watch the cork fly in the air. Well, when setting up this experiment he thought the tighter the cork the higher it would fly, but in reality the cork stayed and the glass jug blew apart. Ray and I had glass splinters in our shirts but Ed had glass splinters in his face and mainly in his forehead. Fortunately, there was no glass splinters in his eyes. His mother removed most of the glass with tweezers. Week's later small pieces of glass were surfacing around his forehead and as he would pick them out he would say, "Well there's another one". After time they disappeared.

Most of our escapades around the creek, river, Cambridge woods, and Dredge Harbor were during summer vacation when school was out. We spent a lot of time fishing, swimming and canoeing. When we were a little older we made pocket money washing boats at Dredge Harbor. Ray & I also helped Ed launch boats for Mr. Parsons.

During the boat building days in Delanco my mother's Uncle, Howard Wills, came to my father with the proposition of building a boat. Howard started fishing on the Rancocas Creek for Shad and Sturgeon, selling them at the Philadelphia Docks across the Delaware. He had a propensity for boats and at times would sit and sketch fishing boats and pleasure boats. Howard would be known as an entrepreneur today as he was always on the go.

In the late 1920's Howard had hired my father to build single family homes down at the shore where he had purchased a large parcel of land. He also opened a grocery store in Riverside, Wills Market. My mother worked at the store for a short time. Uncle Howard was a family man and no matter how busy he always had time for us. I can remember when he came to our house to see my father he always had a pleasant way about himself.

The country was in a deep depression and Uncle Howard was on a mission to help my mother and father make ends meet. We were a family of five at this time and the boat building project put food on the table and paid the rent. Howard lived on Rancocas Ave. in Delanco, N.J. and had a wife, Agnes and (7) seven children. He was in the process of building a home and a business in Delran. My father went over to Delanco to check out the boat plans that were spread out on Howard's dining room table. It didn't take long for my father to take the job as he needed the money and fell in love with this boat from the start.

It wasn't long before the keel was laid on the banks of the Rancocas Creek, 1000 ft. west of the Delanco Bridge. When my father came home to Riverside Park, he made it a point to explain to me each part of the boat he had worked on that day. When the keel was in place he took me over to Delanco and made sure I knew what a keel looked like, and also the type of wood it was made of, which was yellow pine. Then when the ribs were in place, it was the same scenario. I had to see and know that each rib was made of oak.

My father was fascinated with Howard's mathematical skills and how he made the patterns for all the ribs in the boat. The patterns were made in the house and brought out to the job where my father would reproduce them in oak, then fastened them to the keel. When the ribs were all in place the planking was next. There was a series of bracing on the inside of the ribs to hold them in place while the planking was installed. The planking was 1x6 or 1x8 and about 10 ft. long and made of Douglass Fir. Each piece had to be placed in a steam box where it was saturated with steam for a period of time until it was pliable enough to fit the curvature of the boat. The steam box was about 12 inches on the inside and 12 ft. long, and sat up 36 inches off the ground. The lid was made in three sections, 4ft. each, with rubber gaskets.

The steam was produced from a 55 gallon drum which sat high enough so as to build a wood fire underneath. There was a pipe connecting the drum to the steam box. As they place a board in the box, close the lids and latch them, put 2 or 3 gallons of water in the drum, start a fire and as the steam pressure built up in the drum it would transfer by pipe to the box which had a few small holes in the bottom to vent the condensation. After a period of time the board was removed from the box and could easily be bent to fit the shape of the boat.

After the planking and the inside was finished there was an engine compartment about 18 inches high, with doors that opened from the top. Inside were two 8 cylinder Packard engines. The stern was finished in mahogany with the name (Seagull) plainly painted on the back. The top decks were all mahogany. She was 46 ft. long with a 15 ft. beam and weighed 15 ton. The finished coat of white paint was dry and now it came time to make small pencil marks on both sides of the boat to show where the waterline would be painted. This process was very important. It was a black stripe about 2 inches wide and went from the front all the way to the back and the pencil marks were made by Howard. My father painted these stripes exactly on the marks. As far as my father was concerned the job was done but there was one more thing. He looked at Howard and asked. "Where did you get the name Seagull?" Howard answered, "Because I expect this boat to fly."

The date for the launching had finally come, September 7, 1936. It was Labor Day and a little over 100 spectators showed up. Among the spectators were a number of boat builders from Delanco. They were there for one reason, and one reason only, that was to see if the Seagull would float perfectly on its waterline. The boat was launched on the banks of the Rancocas creek and there were only two men on the boat. Howard at the helm and his nephew, Bud Richter, on the bow of the boat. Howard gave the signal and the chocks were kicked out and the Seagull slipped into the water. Howard fired up the engines and backed up toward the bridge as he told Bud to throw the anchor over. With the engines idling and the rope stretched tight at the bowl the Seagull was perpendicular to the shore and the spectators. When she settled down perfectly on her waterline, a loud cheer went up from the crowd and Howard knew what this meant.

My father was pleased that everything turned out just as he expected. After a few weeks, while the weather was nice, Uncle Howard took our family out on the Delaware River and opened the throttle so we could experience what he meant, when he said the Seagull would fly. It was unbelievable how these 46 ft. cabin cruisers could sail along the water. Howard had a good time cruising and fishing on the Seagull for about 5 years and then the Second World War came along; at this time the Coast Guard began looking for registered boats of a certain size. They contacted Howard and made an appointment to look the Seagull over. My father was there the day they arrived. He said they went over the boat taking measurements and writing reports. When they finished they told Howard he would hear from them.

It wasn't long before they were back and said they would like to commission the Seagull for the duration of the war to patrol the coast along Atlantic City. There was only one answer; it was an honor to have your boat chosen to serve with the US Coast Guard. Howard was proud to sign the papers which stated the boat would be returned after the war in the same condition. They photographed the Seagull and in a few days the Coast Guard took command and they sailed west up the Rancocas Creek and south down the Delaware River.

She served our country well and when the war was over she returned in beautiful condition just like the day she left, but with one difference; the twin Packard engines were replaced with twin Gray Diesel Engines. This was 1946 and Howard was through with boating. He turned the boat over to his brother, Tom, for a modest sum and his brother Tom used it for fishing parties and made a good living out of it.

My father started to keep track of her as he was proud of the Seagull. She was like family to us. After a few years, she was sold to a buyer in Florida. My father communicated by letter with each one of these owners all the way up to 1960. Then she disappeared. He suspected she was lost in the Bay of Pigs fiasco. He tried for years to find her but with no success I guess I'm still living with those memories myself.

After my father finished building the Seagull he built a roadside stand or market for Howard on the northbound side of Rt.130, in Bridgeboro N.J. All the sons and daughters worked there selling fruits and vegetables. It was a well known market in its time. Howard had a large piece of land behind the roadside stand were he built homes for each one of his family which included 5 daughters, 2 sons, and their spouses. This section of Bridgeboro was known to the family as "Willsville" and is still there today. The Wills family moved to this location in Delran late in 1936. Uncle Howard retired and spent the rest of his days in Florida with the exception of a few trips to Jersey to see his family. He always stopped to see my father. Uncle Howard was a big part of our family and we miss him, God bless his soul.

While we lived on Stewart Ave., my father developed a set of high speed fed rolls for small and some medium size punch presses. There were a great number of punch press companies in this county and they fed flat metal stripes into the press and punched out small parts. This was 1936 and the punching speed was about 150 pieces per minute.

With the Klingler high speed rolls the speed increased to 500 pieces per minute. He received a U.S. Patent that year and signed up with a company who paid royalties. I've seen small punch presses that used this type feed roll system during WWII and I know they helped speed up production which helped the war effort.

Next a small house where Francis Bart and his wife Madelyn lived. While living here, he went to work for the New York Shipbuilding Corp. in Camden, N.J. His wife Madelyn was a classy lady, well dressed and very mannerly. She was the love of his life and without her I really don't know what would have happened to my good friend Francis Bart. They moved to a new house in Riverton where he spent his retirement years working a part time job as a bar tender and going home sober. Strange things do happen and I'm glad it happened to a guy with a big heart.

Across the street were two big guys, Charles 'Buck" Volkman and his brother, Gus Volkman. Both worked for PSE&G and I really can't remember either one of them having children. They lived next door to each other even after retirement. You will always meet these types of people in a community, unassuming but yet dedicated to the neighborhood. Both Charlie and Gus were members of the Delran Fire Company and their wives as well. There were no through streets between Stewart and Alden Avenues. This was probably the longest block in town. It began at River Road and continued all the way down to the Rancocas Creek.

Here's why I speak so kindly of these two Volkman families. The back of their properties met with the Fire House property, and for 20 plus years, when the siren sounded, they allowed any and all firemen to access the firehouse from Stewart and Chester Ave. In later years Burge St. was cut through from Stewart to Alden, but even then, there was no fencing behind the Volkman's property and for some years the firemen continued to cut through the back yards. After a number of years the only one left was Gus Volkman's wife, Emma. She lived there until she was 90 and then sold the house and moved to an apartment in Hunters Glen Apartment Complex. She made many trips to the casino up into her late 90's and lived to the age of 106.

The Myer's family also lived here in the first block of Stewart Ave. Isn't it ironic that all three families, the Myer's, Klingler's, and Siegfried's, also lived on the same block in Riverside, now live on the same block in Delran ?. My parents added two more to the family, my brothers, Francis and Wayne. And the Myers added two, Fred and Ruth. Fritz was a painter. That seems to explain it all, but not so. He was more than just a painter, he was a husband, a father, a good hearted friend, a self employed business man with the skills of a contractor.

He would go to a home and assist the owner in a color scheme, do the mathematical calculation in square feet, arrive at the amount of paint per gallons needed to do the job and hire extra help as needed. A painter / contractor back then had to be an alchemist. He started with a mixture of white lead, a color pigment, linseed oil, and turpentine, not to mention preparing the interior and exterior surfaces of a building before the painting could be started. Fritz had three daughters and a son Fred. Fred and I were lifetime friends, we went to school together and kept in touch most of our lives.

Harry and Hazel Stevenson raised a family here in Riverside Park. Hazel was a member of the ladies Auxiliary and Harry was a driver and pump operator for the Fire Co. They lived across the street from the (Volkman's). If the siren sounded 3'clock in the morning, Harry would jump out of bed, pull his pants on and slip into his shoes, run through the back yards, and at times be the first one at the fire house. You have to know Harry, like I knew Harry. He was a man of determination, born in Beverly, N.J. and contracted Polio as a young kid. His mother passed away at a young age and Harry was sent to live with his married sister, Frances Miller, (nee) Stevenson.

Harry wore braces on both legs and it is hard to imagine him running to the firehouse but believe me he did, many times. He worked odd jobs for awhile then found his nitch when he landed a job with an Electro Plating Co. in Camden N.J. Then two things happened to Harry, first, he became able to walk without his leg braces, and second, he enrolled in a trade school for electro plating which involved a lot of chemistry. He did well at this trade and when WWII started he was not eligible for the service so he applied for a defense job at the New York Shipbuilding Co. in Camden. They placed him in the Electrical Department which had a large plating room. He worked there as a supervisor until the day he retired.

Harry was also a drummer with John Smith on the accordion as I played guitar. We played as a trio for "The Park" fire house for many years. At times, while playing for weddings, we would add a musician or two. We played for a lot of clubs and fire houses around the area. One of the jobs we enjoyed was at "POP'S SHORE BAR" on Long Beach Island. We played there on opening night, four years in a row.

The Park Community Church had a profound effect on the young people of this community over the years. The founder, Reverend Hundsinger, worked for PSE&G. He and his family kept the church going. Most of the young kids in the neighborhood went there for Sunday School Lessons, including myself. After Reverend Hundsinger passed away, Bill Lipinski, who was a student of theology, kept the church going with the help of his family, which we'll speak about later.

To the right side of the Church lived the Williamson family, John Williamson worked for the Riverside Metal Works Co. as a supervisor in the machine shop, and with his recommendation, I received a job at the machine shop. In later years this property was bought by the Park Community Church, with the house as a parsonage.

Next, the P.C. Klingler general machine shop, where I served my apprenticeship. Paul was my uncle, my father was shop foreman. There were four machinist plus six machine operators working there at the time. Paul and my father both held U.S. Patents. They seemed to be inventors by nature. Paul worked at Billy Traubel's Hosiery Mills in his early days and developed a braking system that would stop the hosiery knitting machines when they broke a needle. These machines had 50 or more needles and when one needle broke it would take out quite a few more with it. Sometimes, all of the needles would go. The braking system could stop the machine if just one needle broke, saving money for the hosiery industry. He sold quite a few of these "stop motions" to the hosiery industry.

He also owned the lot between him and the Schmidt's house where later my grandmother had a house built for her and my great-grandmother. She sold her house on Alden Ave. to Joe Makin. When he moved, Harry and Frances Miller bought the half of the double from Joe. This included a lot the size of a ¼ acre. In later years their daughter Shirley married Joe Majewski, Harry and Frances transferred this lot as a wedding gift for the newlyweds. Joe worked as a union carpenter out of Philly. He and a few of his friends built a Cape Cod house on this lot. Joe's gone, sad to say, but his son, Glen, and wife, Peggy, still live there.

Joe Makin was a C.P.A. (certified public accountant) and did most of the bookkeeping for a lot of the small businesses around town. Joe and Edna had two children, Joan and Donald, who attended Cambridge Elementary School here in Delran. Joan was one of those attractive girls that made the boys heads spin. Even today, when her name is mentioned, Joan and Beautiful are Synonymous. Donald still lives in Delran. He is a handsome and reserved type of guy, just like his father. Their mother, Edna Makin, always dressed well, like a movie star, "that's my opinion." She loved her Boston terrier bull dogs and I can still see her taking them for a walk on a long leash. It is one of those pictures that stay with you for a life time.

Ernie and Evelyn Hess bought the right side of this double house after the Parkers moved out and raised a daughter and two sons. Barbara, Melvin, and Ernie Jr. My brother, Wayne, married Barbara and they live in New Hampshire. We bought the Millers side of this double in the early 60's; we became part of the Hess family. Ernie Sr. and Evelyn were the nicest neighbors one could have. We enjoyed them while they were here.

Now, here's an interesting story. The Schmidt family, Philip Schmidt worked at Taubel's hosiery mill. Back then William Taubel was known as the King of full fashion hosiery in the world. He had hosiery mills in other towns and cities in the U.S.A. While working there Philip got caught in a piece of machinery and lost an arm. William Taubel gave him a lifetime job as a night watchman. William Taubel liked his employees to call him Billy, and I know there are newspapers and books from the past that refer to him as Billy Taubel, and you can see in this one situation how Billy Taubel treated his employees. Philip's wife was a professional whistler. She whistled on a radio station in Philadelphia and she would whistle songs and bird calls. As kids we would get up close to the back fence to hear her whistle while she hung out the cloths.

Bill & Gertie Kalmes lived in the first half of this double house across from the Schmidt family. They had two daughters Connie, Carron, and a son Bill. Bill Sr. worked as a union carpenter out of Philadelphia and had three hobbies, fishing, hunting, and baseball. Gertie was born and raised in Chatsworth. Bill spent a lot of time fishing and hunting in the area, often frequenting the stores in Chatsworth. I supposed he and Gertie met at one of these establishments, started dating and later married moving to Stewart Ave. in 'The Park".

Bill was well known for catching snappers and in the fall when the Fire Company had their annual dinner, Bill Kalmes would supply the snappers for the ladies auxiliary famed homemade snapper soup. Bill was also well known for his baseball career in the Burlington County league. They nick named him "Wild Bill Kalmes" and he held the league record for wild pitches. Most of the batters would back off the plate if they knew what was good for them. He pitched from 1929 to 1960. He was 14-4 in 1940 and 10-1 in 1947. He also had a back- to- back 32- strikeout performance in 1942. In 1957 Wild Bill and his son Bill Kalmes Jr. led the pitching staff for the Riverside Bombers. Young Bill struck out 164 batters in 104 innings in 1956, the next year he led Riverside Bombers to the county championship with a 12-3 record. He struck out a record 189 in 119 innings. Bill senior served as a reliever and starter. Young Bill Kalmes signed a contract that took him through the Los Angeles Dodgers' organization. This father and son combination was hard to beat. Thanks to Bob Kenney for these statistics as he just happened to be the manager of the Riverside Bombers in those early years.

The other half of this double house lived William (Dur) Horner and his wife, Betty. They had three sons and two daughters. Everyone in this family dedicated most of their spare time to the service of the Riverside Park Fire Co. and the Emergency Squad. Dur served as the recording secretary for the fire company and also served as a police officer here in "The Park". He worked full time at the Riverside Metal Company. In later years he worked as the township clerk. Betty and her daughters served in the Park Fire Co. Ladies Auxiliary and we still have some of her recipes. She was one among several great cooks with "The Park" Fire Company; the boys served as firemen and officers, also doing a fine job over the years. Don Horner is working with the Emergency Squad as a senior officer as I write.

There is a small house belonging to the Sooy family. I never knew them by their first names, but there seemed to be an interesting mix-up in the deed for this property as its boundary included quite a few properties in this area. For one reason or another Mr. Sooy's deed gave him ownership of a large section of Riverside Park. The banks and mortgages Co. had to send an agent out with a document that had to be signed by each home owner whose property was included in this deed. The last thing they had to do was to confront Mr. Sooy, hoping he would understand. It turned out that he was a very congenial man and signed the release papers making the banks and his neighbors happy. A few years prior to this incident their young son, George, was struck and killed by a fast moving train. I'm almost sure he was on his bicycle and tried to beat the train at Alden Avenue crossing.

Charlie Shinn moved his trucking business from St. Mihiel Dr. to Stewart Ave. and later sold this property to George Gilbert, then later built a house across the street. George Gilbert built two houses here in 1950 and became a lifelong member of the Riverside Park Vol. Fire Company. At that time, Ed Iwanicki, I and George Gilbert worked on the addition to the back of the old fire house which gave the ladies auxiliary a larger kitchen. That's when I found out that George Gilbert could work. This man loves work and hasn't missed one day since.

The Clarkson's, Esworthy's and Hunter's were next. Bill Clarkson worked for the Radio Condenser Co. in Camden N.J. as an electrical engineer. His hobby was fishing and boating. We watched him build an 18 ft. fishing boat in his back yard and when it was finished he had to remove part of the neighbor's fence so as to bring the boat out to Stewart

Ave. His neighbor, John Esworthy, was a little disturbed at the time but Bill made sure the fence was back where it belonged and everyone was happy. Bill's daughter, Norma, was also a class mate who was a horse lover. Most of her time was spent riding and taking care of her prized horse. Whenever we walked home from school and arrived at Stewart Ave., we could hear that horse bellowing, knowing Norma was on her way home. She later married and moved to Florida and as far as I know she still has horses.

Jack Esworthy was raised here by his father and stepmother, Edna. Jack was very young when his mother passed away. Jack Esworthy, Sr. was a model train enthusiast and he had a spare bedroom dedicated to this year round hobby. I remember visiting with Jack during the Christmas holidays. That's when this model train's exhibit was in full swing. Mr. Esworthy was so meticulous about each piece of scenery as there were railroad crossings, loading docks, tunnels, houses and churches. There were streets with little cars and lamp posts. You could walk around three sides. The one side was against the wall and Mr. Esworthy would remind us not to touch anything even though we knew that beforehand.

Jack would always complain about his father not letting him operate the trains. When Jack became old enough and responsible enough to take good care of these trains his father turned everything over to him, and I know for a fact that each piece was well taken care of. Mr. Esworthy worked in the power plant for PSE&G in Burlington, N.J. Jack followed in his father's footsteps and worked there until he retired. Jack enlisted in the U.S.M.C. during the Second World War and when he was discharged he went right back to work for PSE&G. Now, Jack lives in Florida with quite a collection of antique model trains.

Alma Hunter lived next door. She played the piano in every club in town. She was known for her exuberant style on the ivories and at times you would think the piano was going to leave the floor. What a musician She had that Joann Castle style of playing. Her son, Roy, was a vocalist and sang with a lot of bands in the area. I remember seeing him perform with a band at Turners Hall one night. A patron had requested Roy's impression of Frank Sinatra and that famous style. Roy stepped up on the stage and removed his jacket and slung it over his right shoulder and as he walked up to the mic he removed the cigarette from his mouth and let out a puff of smoke, and began to sing Frank Sinatra's signature song, "Put Your Dreams Away for Another Day". You would think Frank just walked in the door. It wasn't just his demeanor, he had the voice to go with it, and being a vocalist and musician myself I was interested in his delivery. In my humble opinion, I think he nailed it that night. I've always been a Bing Crosby fan and that was my style of singing, however, that goes back a few years.

There was a large section of ground on the opposite side of the street. If you looked toward Alden Ave., part of this ground belonged to the township and part to the Lipinsky family who donated their share to the township. At the present time it has a name, "Friendship Park and Play Ground".

Fred Wolff Jr. bought a house next to Friendship Park and still lives here as I write. He spent his childhood living and being raised next to the Park Fire House, with his two sisters, Gale and Joan. His father, Fred Sr. was known for his artistic ability on oil paintings. His restoration of chips and cracks on fine china and antique lamps was undetectable. In fact, some of his work was done for the Smithsonian Institute in Washington D.C. His wife, Claire, was a large part of Fred's endeavors. They were like a team made in Heaven, him with his art history and research, and Claire with her secretarial skills writing newspaper articles and corresponding with the Smithsonian Institute.

When I think of his oil paintings there's one that stands out in my mind, and that's the "Old Boathouse" at the end of Chester Ave. on the banks of the Rancocas Creek. In his early days while working on oil paintings of the 1880 New York Slums he caught the "history bug" which helped steer him into the history of his hometown Delran. 1880 was also the date Delran was incorporated into the County of Burlington. It wasn't long before Fred was painting historical pictures of Burlington and Delran. His interest grew to the point that he became a member of the town council then became Delran Historian in 1972.

Another of his most famous paintings that takes in the history of this area is the "Post Rider." Fred incorporated one of the old historical buildings of Delran as a background with the Post Rider, his swift horse with a leather mail bag attached to the saddle in the foreground. The Post Rider, according to Fred, who studied each of his subjects before capturing them on canvas, said that the Post Rider appeared in New Jersey around 1740 carrying the mail from Philadelphia to New York via Bridgeboro. He would stop here, put the mail on a flat boat and carry it across the Rancocas Creek to another rider waiting on the shore who would continue on to Burlington. Travelers soon began to accompany the post rider who would guide and also entertain them with his stories and bits of news. Soon, overnight accommodations were needed before the difficult crossing at the Rancocas Creek. These accommodations were made at the Bridgeboro Tavern which was built in 1733 and later came the authorization of a ferry to cross the creek in 1747, shortly after the construction of the Burlington and Camden Pike, which is now Rt. 130.

Fred attributes his talents to his mother who earned money during the depression years by using her artistic ability to paint floral scenes on dishes, vases and glassware. Fred worked along with her in his early days and became quite an artist on his own. He entered a contest for art school and won a scholarship which he couldn't afford. Then he was offered a job as an apprentice engineer at a power plant for a laundry in Philadelphia Pa. He held this job for years while pursuing his childhood hobby which was making lamps from all types of materials including railroad lanterns, baseball bats, artillery shells, antique telephones, coffee mills, buffalo hoofs, you name it.

He continued painting portraits of historical buildings, churches, and bridges and also displayed more than 30 of his paintings at the Mount Holly Art Center and sidewalk exhibit on High Street. Fred also became Vice President of the Burlington County Art Guild. In 1968 Fred opened The Wayside Art Gallery at Rt. 130 and Fairview St. in Delran. Now he could devote more time to the business. His wife, Clair, helped with the shop and also made all the lamp shades. She put her artistic talent on every lampshade in the gallery. During the Second World War Fred served as director of civil defense and chief air raid warden. He notes that during the 40's Delran had a three man council. These members were, Lee Haines, William Kauderer and Frank Yansick who was also the first Chief of Police with two part time officers. Raymond Litle was the Township Clerk. Over the years Fred Wolff has served on the planning board, the economical development group and the cultural committee.

He was commissioned in the late 60's to design a seal for the township to celebrate the bicentennial of the Declaration of Independence. In 1976 the seal was affixed to mugs and certificates and published for the township's sponsored banquets and award ceremonies. Later Fred was approuched about using this seal for a township flag and he agreed. He went to work and in a few weeks presented his flag to the council. They accepted it and in a month or two it was flying in front of the Municipal building. Fred was elated to say the least. In 1980 Fred was named Grand Marshal of the parade celebrating Delran's 100 Anniversary. How much more can you say about a man who served his family, his country and his community leaving a history depicted in paintings and a long lasting township flag and seal?

A little farther down Stewart Ave. lived Charles and Margret Heck. They had three sons, Marvin, who worked for RCA as personnel director, Robert, who worked as a contractor/supervisor for PSE&G, and Richard, a biology teacher at Pennsauken High School. This family was a joy and a pleasure to know. Marge was the quintessential housewife, mother, and homemaker, dedicated to her family and also her neighbors. If she knew someone in need, she felt a responsibility to help, and she raised her three sons in the same way.

Marvin and I went to Cambridge School along with others in the neighborhood and at times walked the same path home. We would talk about our hobbies which were quite different but the same within our families. Marvin loved sports and my passion was music. I tried playing baseball but just couldn't hack it. My brother, Fran, could do both and my brother, Wayne, had the real gift for music. Marvin's brother, Richard, played the accordion and at times when I stopped in to see

Marvin Richard would be practicing the accordion. I guess that's the way I got acquainted with the family.

I always thought their mother, Marge, was a Registered Nurse by profession but opted out like many other women to become a homemaker. If neighboring kids got a small cut on their finger one of the sons would bring them in through the kitchen door and Marge was always there to mend their wounds and dry their tears, if any. Their father, Charlie, worked 40 years for Bell Telephone of Philadelphia, Pa. He was also a charter member of the Riverside Park Fire Company and participated in minstrel shows to raise money for the fire company.

Marvin and Bob became members of the "Jersey Joe's" American Legion Senior Drum & Bugle Corp, which were National Champion at the time. They were established in 1946, became National Champions in 1948 and continued on until 1955. During the Korean War Bob Heck enlisted in the US Navy and after serving a few years returned home. He enrolled in mechanical drawing classes at the Spring Garden Institute in Philadelphia and received his degree in mechanical drafting.

Now here's some bad luck for Marvin and his passion for sports. We must go back a few years when Riverside had a semipro football team that was known as the "Riverside Big Green". Between the late 1930's and early 1940's two other Riverside teams named the Greyhounds and the Eagles had disbanded. It was now that the dreamed of having another semipro football team came to fruition, in 1941. A handful of guys from Riverside formed this club and named it Blair A.C. in honor of mentor Earl "Blair" Edge. They played one season then World War II came along and most of the young boys went off to serve their country. With this shortage of players they decided to look to Riverside Park for football players, most of who were now playing for Palmyra High School. Some of the guys I mentioned prir had joined the team, namely, Hermie Klemm, Bill Steedle, Marvin Heck, Whitey Bembow, and Frank Breuer.

It so happened that during one of the games when Marvin dove for a fumbled ball, his arm went over top of the ball and a player from the opposing team landed on him breaking Marvin's forearm in (5) five places. He was taken to a local hospital where they treated him by setting his arm and placing a cast from his elbow down to the wrist. He came home very disappointed, his arm in a sling and the thought he would not play football again. Little did he know this was the least of his problems?

Eventually he realized the scope of this accident. His arm had to be broken and reset numerous times. Each time they removed part of the bone they placed pins and plates and screws to hold the bone together. After several years and many operations Marvin continued with his life, his right arm shorter than his left with some limited movement. I did notice that when he was around strangers he kept his right-hand in his pocket. He probably didn't want to go through a lengthy explanation.

After finishing high school Marvin went to work for RCA Victor in Camden, N.J. and in time became Personnel Director. To this day, I remember Marvin saying to me, "If you ever need a job come see me." Marvin's gone now and when I think back, we were like brothers and his thoughtfulness is still with me.

Ernie Taylor was one of the first to be drafted during the Second World War. His parents didn't want to see him go for he was their only son, their only child, the only one they loved with all their heart and soul. By now, you probably know what's coming next; a knock on the door and when Mrs. Taylor opened the door, two Army officers were standing there. All of a sudden her knees buckled and one of the officers helped her to a chair. They were there to inform her that her son, Ernie, was killed in action.

He was with an armored division going into the German's front line. When the Sherman tank he was in became disabled by enemy fire, Ernie jumped from the tank and into a ditch with rifle in hand and began firing. An enemy hand grenade lobed into the ditch, went off, and another combat soldier, Ernie Taylor, lost his life fighting for the things he and all of us believe in. Mr. & Mrs. Taylor didn't want to leave the house and kept themselves secluded from the outside world. Then one day they just packed up and moved. There were a few neighbors who knew where they relocated, but respected the Taylor's right to grieve in their own way. It's a sad situation that never left us completely. Ironically, Fred Pfeffer Sr., a very close friend of Ernie's, had a nightmare a week before Ernie was killed. Fred dreamed that Ernie was running into battle when he was hit by enemy fire. Fred, in a cold sweat, sat straight up in bed. He said it was hard sleeping after that, especially when Ernie's death became a reality. These are the kind of war stories that shake a person to the core.

Chet Beuker as a young man decided to join the CCC during the great depression. This was one of the programs that President Roosevelt set in motion to make work for young men. There were a lot of acronyms for these programs, for instance; WPA, TVA, and for the "CCC" it was the acronym for the Civilian Conservation Corp. These men were dedicated to building camp sites in the national forest thereby cleaning out the brush around the trees making the environment friendlier for everyone. This was the beginning of the National Park Service which we enjoy today.

Later Chet had a sense of emergency. He could see that the Second World War was coming our way and was about to enlist in the US Army. But first he had to have a second opinion. Maybe a buddy system would help him along. So, he went to see his good friend Julius Klingler and asked him to go along with his plan. Julius agreed and they both went off to the Army Recruiting Office. Well, as it so happened, Chet passed the physical and Julius didn't. Chet became a Major in the US Army and made it his career.

My uncle Julius Klingler, decided to join the N.J. State Police. He was accepted and this was his carrier until he retired. The following is worth mentioning. During the Lindbergh kidnapping case, Uncle Julius was one of three State Police officers stationed at the Lindbergh house to take incoming phone calls around the clock. I can remember him talking to my father about the Lindbergh case, but I couldn't hear what was said.

Bill Breuer, Sr. and his wife, Karolina, had seven children, three daughters and four sons. Bill also had a poultry farm and in later years had his own candy business. He was a confectioner by trade. Bill and Karolina formerly lived in Philadelphia. After they were married they moved to Riverside Park. This is where they remained for the rest of their days.

During his early days, while being employed by a large candy manufacturer in the city of Philadelphia Pa. this company not only produced fine candies for local retailers, they also shipped these fine products over to Europe where they were well received.

Bill was a very resourceful man and as his family grew he decided to start a part-time business at home. Most of the residents in this area had small backyards with a few chickens. Bill had over an acre of ground. His property stretched back at least 400 feet from the house. Little by little he built these long chicken houses and purchased a number of chicks that were known as "leghorns".

As the egg business grew the chickens began laying more eggs. Bill began selling eggs by the crate to wholesalers. In the early years Delran was known as a farming community and the competition in eggs sales grew rapidly. This left Bill with some new choices. He slowly moved away from the egg business and began building a candy factory. Yes, this was the business he knew quite well. After all he was a confectioner by trade. I can remember Bill coming to the Klingler Machine Shop where I worked at the time. There were occasions when he needed machine work on his candy making machines. Anytime he brought a part or a piece of machinery to the shop it was usually my job to repair or replace the item since I knew what had to be done. I assure you; he was a satisfied customer and always returned.

In later years Frank Breuer, Bills son, and I were talking about the candy factory He said he had just gathered up all the candy making machines and gave them to a local candy company. He asked nothing in return. This was typical Frank Breuer who was always willing to give and never looking to receive.

His brother, Bill, went on to college and later married. He went into the building trades. He also pursued and obtained a private pilot's license. He and his wife raised three children. The last time I talked to him he was happily retired. There were three Breuer's that I knew very well, Harry, Frank, and Caroline. We went to Cambridge School at the same time. When Harry finished school he went to work for Rundles in Pennsauken. He suffered with cancer and died at the age of 52. I'm sure it was job related.

Caroline married Richard Scholzewski. He was a self employed fine cabinet maker. Frank and I were the closest. After we finished school I started my trade as an apprentice machinist and Frank became an Ironworker. He was a lifetime member of the Ironworkers Local #68 out of Trenton, N.J. He worked on high rise buildings and also worked on the Causeway Bridge going to Long Beach Island.

Frank and I hung out together quite a bit. One day, when I was at the house, Frank said, "Let's go horseback riding." Well, when we got there he insisted on paying. So the stable boy came out with two horses. Frank put his left foot in the stirrup and threw his right leg over the saddle. At the same time I was attempting to get my foot in the stirrup. When I finally landed in the saddle the horse reared up and threw me off his back. I hit the ground while the horse took off running. One of the workers jumped on a horse and made chase.

In the mean time they brought out another horse for the less experienced. They helped me in the saddle and off we went. My horse, with his head down, and Frank sitting high on a beautiful tan horse. I can tell you that Frank never laughed as he was more concerned that I may have gotten hurt. I had a sore butt for a week, yet no one ever knew.

In a few years Frank married Grace Myers and bought a house on the first block of Stewart Ave. Here they raised four children. It seemed as though Frank always had a boat and a fishing pole. Just before he retired he purchased a 38 ft. sail boat. Before long, he and Grace were sailing down to the Bahamas.

Frank would talk about how they went from one island to another, stay for a brief time then sailed on. He had acquired a good bit of knowledge sailing through the water ways and wherever he went people would take a liking to him. In this way he gleaned most of the information he needed to travel and stay on different, Islands.

He would return to his home on Stewart Ave. in the fall and keep busy helping his children and his neighbors. He was an all around mechanic and if someone had a problem with their car not starting, or an electrical problem at the house, even a leak in the roof, you name it, and Frank could fix it. The Breuer's had three younger children whom I never got to know.

Frank and I remained friends all of our lives but he's gone now, "To Whence No One Returns". I'm certain he'll be missed by his family friends and neighbors.

Frank Tighe and his wife had two sons, Bud, and Frank, Jr. Both sons went in to the service during WWII. Bud served in the Navy and Frank in the Army. Bud married and divorced shortly after coming home from the service. Frank was a prisoner of war and weighed less than 100 pounds when he returned home. He never married and lived at home. They both went from job to job and continued to drink. It was such a shame that two young brothers who were raised to be gentle and caring neighbors, had now turned into alcoholics. Their mother was a kind and lovely woman. Back then, we didn't know what the problem was, but now it's called PTSD. Their father did everything he could to help in this tragic situation, but the constant drinking just sucked the life out of their two sons. Frank Sr. worked at the Keystone Watch Case Co. in Riverside and hardly ever missed a day's work even though this heavy load was laid on his shoulders. He persevered just like Job in the Old Testament. Frank said that the horrors of war were too much for his sons. Being friendly with the family and especially Frank Jr., it was painful for me and the guys in the neighborhood, to see how Frank and Bud wasted away.

Robert "Scotty" Parker came to this country from Scotland. He was employed by a company that built carriages. He was an artist with fine detailing skills in floral designs with gold leaf and pin striping. If you've ever seen pictures of European carriages with large spoke wheels, these spokes and wheels were highly decorated with pin striped vines and leaves, small flowers, and a touch of gold leaf here and there.

The outside of the carriage was black, with plain pin striping. The inside was gold leaf and pin striping. Scotty worked his way up through the company, and was chosen to detail the carriage belonging to the

Queen of Scotland. This gave him the monetary ability to fulfill his dream in coming to America.

He arrived in the early 1900's with a promise of a job in Riverside. There was plenty of painting to be done around this business district. He moved into a house next to Frank Tighe and started his long career painting signs. He also did gold leaf lettering in windows and on fire trucks. His house was diagonally across the street from the Breuer's house. When Frank got his first car he asked Scotty Parker to do some pin striping around the doors, hood, and trunk. This started a trend with the local guys. They all wanted the same pin striping for their cars and motorcycles. I personally watched Scotty paint Gold Leaf letters on one of our fire trucks.

Bill Kortman, his wife Reba, and Kenneth lived down in the lower part of Stewart Ave. Before there were police officers in Riverside Park, Bill Kortman severed the community as the one and only Constable. He may have been self appointed, who knows. If you approached him straight on he could be very intimidating. He had broad shoulders and always stood his ground, but if you were a friend, you were a friend forever. This was a part time job and he didn't have too many problems with the young guys around town. We all had a good picture of him in the back of our minds. He worked as a machinist for the Riverside Metal works and put in many years before retiring.

Rudolph Gopenner, and his wife, Ellie, also lived on Stewart Ave., with one son, Rudy Jr. Ellie was a wife, mother, and home maker, which was normal back in the 30's and 40's. Now, the woman of the house is called a "domestic engineer", which makes sense. Rudy and Ellie always seemed very congenial. You could tell their character by the way they raised their son, Rudy, Jr. He was friendly and outgoing, the results of being raised in the right way.

Rudy Sr. worked as a maintenance supervisor for the Keekeffer Manufacturing Co. located in Pennsauken, N.J. They made corrugated cardboard for boxes. Then, in the 40's, they transferred Rudy to a plant in Maine where he was back and forth for two years. Now that the job looked permanent, he and Ellie decided it was time to sell and move on.

Even though Rudy came home occasionally, the in between times were lonely times for Ellie. She was more than happy to make a new home in Maine. Eventually young Rudy became part of the company.

Florence Stewart was a very classy lady. She worked in full fashion hosiery in Philadelphia for many years. She lived in one of the two houses that were part of the Stewart Estate. It's the only house on Stewart Ave made of "Brown Stone".

The other house is located at the corner of River Drive and Stewart Avenue. The Stewart Farm occupied this four street area from Chester Avenue to Norman Avenue.

As far as I know, Florence was related to the Stewart family. These two houses are over 150 years old. Florence walked from close to the Rancocas Creek, up to St.Mihiel Drive every morning where she met two other people who worked at the same establishment. It was worthwhile to work for some of these companies in Philadelphia as they paid very well.

Frank Heaton moved to The Park from Bridgeboro. He had enough money to buy a lot, on the lower part of Stewart Avenue. He built a shack and lived there by himself. He was very poor, and the neighbors knew it, but here in Riverside Park, you never had to do without. In the winter they made sure he had firewood and food would come from one house or another. He did odd jobs when he could find them. Frank was a kind soul, and even though he lived in a one room shack, he never lost his dignity.

He would work the ground during the summer planting vegetables of different varieties, sharing some with his neighbors and selling the rest. He came from a farm family and this is what he knew best. The planting season was short and the winters were long, and so the neighbors kept an eye on the wood pile, restocking it now and then. This is the true meaning of community, or neighborhood, as we knew it. One neighbor helping the other. During the 40's and 50's houses were springing up one after the other. I can count at least ten houses on Stewart Ave. alone. There's lore to live near the Rancocas Creek and her beautiful sunsets.

Ted and Annette Jankowski moved here after getting married, I'm most certain it was 1950, they raised two sons and a daughter in "The

Park" and for the most part they were a very reserved family. As members of St. Pete's church in Riverside, and dedicated to their faith, what else can one say about a neighbor?

I never got to know Mr. and Mrs. Eigenbrood, but I did know the two boys, Jimmy and Johnny. They were friends with the Pfeffer boys and the Wigmores. One thing they had in common was boating along the Rancocas Creek. Back then the hydroplane boats were popular. They seemed small for the large outboard motors that powered them. On the weekend you could hear them screaming along the creek. They would even enter racing events at Barnegat Bay. I don't know if there were any winners, but I do know they had the time of their lives. The Eigenbroods' had two other sons I never got to know, Joe and Jerry. Just a guess, but when the four boys got together they were probably thick as thieves.

On the opposite side of Stewart Ave. lived the Jurimas family, Fred & Ruth, who had three boys and twin daughters. They are part of the extended Lipinsky family from Alden Ave. Ruth lost her husband Fred a few years back and when her children had married and left the nest. She found her soul-mate Jim Wentworth, and now they are married, living in "The Park". I must say a fine couple.

The next house belonged to the Workman family. Their daughter still lives on Stewart Ave. She has two brothers, both of whom are married. One lives in "The Park" and the other in Cambridge. Their mother and father live in upstate New York. This family lives up to their sir name. They love to work, and in all the years I've known them, I've never seen one of them in a lounge chair, the word lounge is not in their vocabulary. They love what they do, and they do it well, "Amen."

In the mid 50's, Jimmy Maher became the first police officer in Riverside Park. He had one other officer, William (Dur) Horner, working with him. The police station was setup in the front porch of Jimmy Maher's home; it is the last house on the right hand side #88 Stewart Ave. We had lost our Justice of the peace, John McNulty, in the early 1940's which left a vacancy for a number of years. The town council, which Jimmy was part of, wanted a police station here in "The Park" so Jimmy Maher stepped up to fill the void.

His wife, Mildred, was one of the six Marshall girls who were raised right here in "The Park," on River Drive, between Chester and Stewart. Jimmy also served as Mayor of Delran, to his credit he brought in McMillan & Collier book distributors, which is now Simon & Schuster, who became a huge economic boost to the area. Jim was a very ambitious man and a community type guy he not only did his share, but always had that friendly and neighborly attitude.

This house #88 was previously rented by Arthur States Sr. who had three sons, Bud, George and Arthur Jr. They originally lived in Bridgeboro. That's where Bud, as a young child, was caught in a kitchen fire and scarred for life. One thing I can say about the kids in our class, they all treated Bud as though he had no scars at all. He was always one of us and he knew it. I can't recall what happened to Arthur. Bud moved to Florida and George lives in Riverside. He is 87 and walks 8 to 10 miles a day. He is the happiest guy you'll ever meet! He's a WWII Veteran who served as an Army Ranger during the occupational period of Germany and Austria. A most dangerous job searching buildings for soldiers lost or being held by the Russians, with the thought that a sniper in one of the buildings may have a bullet with your name on it. George became the lead man for this squad of Rangers. The men chose him and trusted him and he never let them down.

On the other side of Stewart Ave. and the last house on the street lived the Nauss family, Bill and his wife Dorothy, and six children, Marian, James, Bill, Dorothy, Jack and Donald. This is the Stewart Farm house that was part of the Stewart Estate; it is well over 150 years old. Having already mentioned the stone house, up the street. The two houses were built more than 20 years before Delran became a township of its own; this area was part of Cinnaminson Township.

The area known as Riverside Park was once the Farm of William Stewart and his family. The only one I can remember is Florence but according to township records there was Thomas, Harry, Alice, and Josephine. The main road to the farm house started at River Road, which is now St.Mihiel Drive, and continued north down to the Rancocas Creek. The farm house is still there at the very end of Stewart Avenue and the Rancocas Creek.

In 1880 the old dirt road was the only road to the farm and was later named "Stewart Avenue." The size of the farm was about four blocks in width from Norman Avenue over to Chester Avenue and somewhat beyond. Mr. Stewart's barn was, as I remember, between Chester Ave. and Whomsley Field.

The township demolished this barn in the 1930's which left a large hill once the barn was gone. This hill was great for sledding during the winter months. It seems that North Chester Ave. didn't exist from River Road down to the Rancocas Creek as this was all farmland and part of William Stewart's Farm.

The population of Riverside was growing fast, and so, in 1895 the State Assembly offset Riverside from Delran making Riverside a new township of its own. Then in 1900 Mr. Stewart was elected to the Township Committee of Riverside for a three year term and served until 1901 and then notified that he was no longer a resident due to the annexation of land during the offset and was being removed from office.

Now with Chester Ave becoming the new dividing line, (Mr. Stewart's Farmhouse was in Delran Township and his Barn in Riverside Township) he protested by moving into his barn in Riverside leaving his family at the farm house. The Township committee of Riverside denied Mr. Stewart's claim sighting the fact that his family was still living in the farm house.

The battle continued until the State Assemble stepped in but not admitting that they were at fault for this whole debacle. Mr. Stewart should have been notified that his property had been compromised by this offset or annexation. The state went out the backdoor, so to speak and found a law of 1899 that stated if any person shall resign from office, or shall die or move out of the township etc. the office shall be deemed to be vacant. A removal by operation of a law, resulting from an act of the legislature cutting off a portion of the township is not deemed to be the fault of the plaintiff. A new ruling was made by the state allowing Mr. Stewart to finish out his three year term in office.

Then in 1916 Riverside Township applied to the County to annex additional land extending from Chester Avenue over to Stewart Avenue. When the two townships voted on the resolution it was lost by one descending vote, that of Mr. Laslocky of Millside Farms. Chester Ave. is still the dividing line today.

Joe and Bonnie Bass purchased this house back in the 50's, Bonnie (nee) Lipinsky was a lifetime member of the Park Community Church. They have two children, Faith and Bill. During their early years they ran a Christian youth program in East Camden with about 175 needy children attending. Bonnie is gone now and Joe still lives in the original Stewart family farm house and keeps it in excellent shape.

He is also the custodian of the church. Joe has a lot of ambition. Sometimes, in the summer, I'll walk across the street to the church and converse with Joe, and maybe give him a hand. On occasions, he'll show his appreciation by bringing over a vase of flowers from the church. Carroll Lipinsky makes all the flower arrangements for the church and she's quite talented. Joe delivers flowers to neighbors who are shut in. He and the Lipinsky family have contributed numerous hours of charitable work for different Christian Missions over the years. Joe worked 37 years for the Cinnaminson School District and is now happily retired.

Part 12

Alden Ave.

Behind my grandmother's house on Alden Ave. lived Mrs. Haywood and her two sons. The one I remember was Lenard, who worked as a plumber. He was really busy when the water and sewer systems were being installed in "The Park" He did a great job for me and many others in our neighborhood.

Directly across the street lived Otto Steinbach and his wife Elisabeth. Otto worked for the Public Service Bus Co. on Pavilion Ave in Riverside. He drove the #9 bus to Philadelphia and back.

Otto was a big man with a nice personality and on, or off the bus, he was always the same. Bus drivers had to be big and strong to handle these buses as there was no power steering just a large wooden steering wheel and hard rubber tires. By the time you arrived in Philadelphia and jumped off that bus you though your teeth wouldn't stop chattering 'til noon. This was a life time job for Otto and he retired and lived quite a few years afterward.

Otto and his wife had no children. His wife, Elisabeth, worked for Bell Telephone as a telephone operator, the kind you would see in an old movie with the big switch board where the operator would ask you what number you wanted and plug you in. She retired after 40 years. She and Otto were very well thought of in the neighborhood. She was Betty Horner's aunt and a lot of us still refer to her as "Aunt Elisabeth". She lived about ten years longer than Otto.

Harley Hankins, his wife, daughter, Sara, and two sons, Henry and Jeanock, lived next to the firehouse. Harley was a charter member and probably served in the fire company for more than fifty years. The siren on top of the firehouse was wired to Harley's house so that when a call came in to the firehouse and a fireman was there, they would take the call and hit the button for the siren. If no one was there the call was transferred to the Hankins house. Harley or Mrs. Hankins would take the call and push the button for the siren setting off the alarm.

There was a tradition here in "The Park". Every night at 7 o'clock Harley would hit a button that would sound the siren one single time and everyone in town would set their clocks and watches. Years later when television became popular Harley would turn on the TV, and when the Lone Ranger came on, it was 7:00 o'clock. The siren would sound and everyone in town knew Harley was watching the Lone Ranger.

He installed a 20 ft. TV tower on top of his two story house with guide wires down to each corner of the roof. More than once, I've seen Harley climb to the top of that tower to make some kind of an adjustment to the TV antenna, making sure the Lone Ranger's picture came in clear. He worked as an auto mechanic for Fortnum motors on Burlington Pike which is now Rt. 130. It seemed like anyone with the name Hankins could take a model T Ford apart and put it back together blind folded.

After the war, Dick Snow built a house diagonally across the street from the firehouse.

He was an active member of the Riverside Park Volunteer Fire Co. and an auto mechanic by trade. He was one of a few mechanics that kept the fire engines in good running condition. There was a push in the neighborhood to start a Boy Scout troop here at the firehouse. At one of the meetings the president asked for a volunteer troop leader. Dick Snow agreed to take the job on a temporary basis, and so Riverside Park Troop #10 got its start.

As soon as I became 12 years of age my mother submitted my name to Dick Snow and the Boy Scouts. Dick was like part of our family. His son, Dick Jr., also joined the Boy Scouts. He and I were like brothers.

Later on, after being married and living in Riverside, Dick Jr. became an officer of the Riverside Turners. I also joined when I was in my 20's. We had a long friendship. Dick and his wife, Case, and daughter, Sherry, worked long hours keeping the Turners operating for a number of years. Dick Sr. was the troop leader for a short time. Where he got the ability to teach is beyond me but he really did a great job. Then, the Second World War came along and Dick joined the Navy. He served for the duration of the war with the Sea Bee's, as Chief Petty officer; He came home in one piece which we were thankful for.

The Riverside Park Volunteer Fire Company #2 began when a handful of citizens decided to purchase a piece of ground large enough to construct a two bay firehouse. It seems that this was the norm for small towns. They needed a fair size pumper truck for house fires and a tank truck for brush fires.

We had donation drives at different times and once a month we ran a social dance. If the dance fell close to a holiday it would be a St. Patty's day dance or a Valentine's dance. The price of admission was fair for a night of music, dancing, food and drinks. Saturday afternoon the trucks were moved out and parked on the side lot. The floors were mopped and tables were setup. I must say, the floors were always kept in fine condition because of the dances and dinners that were held all year long.

When Saturday night arrived and you walked in there were tables around the perimeter and a small table at the entry door where you purchased a ticket. At the left hand corner in the back was a three piece band; Harry Stevenson on Drums, John Smith on the Accordion, and yours truly, Hal Klingler on Guitar and vocals. All three of us were members and donated our time for many Saturday night dances. John Smith was our booking agent. He made sure that our other jobs didn't conflict with the firehouse monthly social dances.

We played for wedding receptions at other firehouses, and local clubs which included Christ-Colombo club, Chiaccio-Club, Riverton Golf-Club, and the Farigate Yacht Club. Once in a while we played for a wedding reception at the Moose Hall. We were busy for fifteen years and had our repeat customers for the social dances at other firehouses. I think we had a fine repertoire from playing at different clubs and weddings; John was great on the accordion.

We played the big band music of the times, also polkas and novelty songs. There was a system of playing two slow songs and then a fast song, followed by a polka or a novelty song; like the Hokey Pokey, Bunny Hop, and the Broom Dance. There were the regular customers from around town but also those from out of town, especially Howard Williams from Pennsauken. He and his wife, their daughter and son in-law, a brother in-law, with his wife and friends would occupy the same table for years. Howard loved to sing and dance. He and his wife were so smooth on the dance floor and every once in a while there would be a request for Howard to come up to the mic and sing. He never failed to entertain. His voice and his timing were perfect in every way; he was a lot of fun.

We also had requests for birthdays and anniversary songs. Sometimes the request would be for special songs that people liked to dance to. Another couple of our friends from Riverside were Claude Stellwag and his wife Floss (nee) Ladzinski. She was originally from Cambridge and her family lived on Main Street. They hardly missed being at the dance with their friends. They would always say hello and asked for their favorite song. These types of friendships last a lifetime.

The ladies auxiliary supplied all of the food for the dances. Halfway through the night the music would stop, and each person would walk up to the counter and carry a paper plate filled with food back to their table. No matter what was served that night, it was always delicious. There were also many great annual dinners where the ladies auxiliary would serve a roast turkey dinner or a roast beef dinner, at which the elected officers were installed.

The firemen held drills at Cambridge School, where we laid fire hose under the railroad track to a fire hydrant across St.Mihiel Dr. We were also on backup call for other fire companies in the district. We participated in a large fire in Riverside when the Fox Theater burnt to the ground; it was a matter of saving the surrounding buildings.

There was also the tragic fire in Lakehurst, NJ when the Hindenburg caught fire and over 30 people lost their lives. A handful of guys hopped on the old Ford pumper with Harry Stevenson driving to Lakehurst to help water down the area. It was a fairly hot scene and pumpers were there from all parts of south Jersey. The Hindenburg was a rigid frame air ship made by the Zeppelin Co. The frame was all aluminum channels with a number of holes spaced apart to lighten up the frame.

I was standing at the corner of St.Mihiel Dr. and Stewart Ave. when Bill Kalmes hopped off the Ford truck on his return home from the Lakehurst fire. He was holding this bright shining piece of aluminum channel, about two inches wide and a foot long, with a series of holes to make it lighter. No one would speak of this afterwards as there were supposed to be no souvenirs. Whatever happened to it no one knows. You would never confront Bill Kalmes, he was not someone to trifle with. Even though he and I were good friends, I never mentioned the Hindenburg souvenir.

The Riverside Park Firehouse was the polling place for the first ward voters and in later years moved to the municipal building. Three of the women that were always there working the polls were Bess Pfeffer, Marian Haines, and Florence Kempista. Marian is gone now but the last time I voted at the municipal building, Florence was still there working for the first ward. It's always nice when we find special people in the community that are there when we need them.

In the late part of 1945 Joe Raphael formed a committee that was known as "The committee of nine" which consisted of Joe as chairman and eight other members. Dick Snow, Max Berkowitz, William (Dur) Horner, Chase Atkinson, Jimmie Maher, Ray Jauss, Nick Valenti, and George Gilbert. Their goal was to acquire a (1950 Buick ambulance) from the Riverside American Legion, then house it at the Riverside Park Firehouse where the above members were in the process of starting an emergency squad.

A friend of mine and a dedicated fireman, George Myers, who lives in Cambridge shared with me his enthusiasm for antique fire trucks, and to my surprise he had the Seagrave fire truck that once belonged to the Riverside Park Fire Company stored in his garage. He purchased this truck after a lengthy search that took him out to Ohio; He drove it back to Delran where he completely restored it to its original condition.

George also has the manufacture's paperwork and pictures which had to be approved by the township before this truck was purchased. George now belongs to a group of firemen in Vineland, N.J. that restores and houses some eleven fire trucks. Each year when the firemen's convention comes along, you'll always see these antique fire trucks and their proud owners in these annual parades.

The Davenport family lived close to the fire house and dedicated a good part of their time as volunteer firemen. Norman and his son, Norman Jr., and Shirley, Norman's wife, served in the Ladies auxiliary. Norman worked at least 35 years for Obergfeild heating oil and service. This company was around for a long while and served oil throughout Riverside, Delanco, and Delran. Not too long after Norman retired Obergfeild closed the business.

Then Todd Meenin built his home on Alden Ave. He was an avid boatman, especially sailboats. He belonged to the Riverton Yacht Club and made this his hobby. At the time, the Lippincott family was building sailboats in Riverton. They were famous for the sailboat they designed and built named the "STAR". This is one of the boats Todd was interested in. The Star was built exclusively for racing and won quite a few international races. Riverton has had sailboat racing along the River Bank every 4th of July for as long as I can remember, one could always spot this sailboat by looking at the very top of the sail. There was a bright red star, with two curved lines at the back, making it look like a shooting star.

When Todd built this house it had the look of a sail in some respects. It had an "A" roof that started at the back of the house and came forward to the front. Half of the front left side jetted out about six feet from the rest of the building. The "A" roof continued on the left side, but on the right side, instead of having the other side of the "A", it had a curvature resembling a sail. It still catches my attention when I drive by.

Lawrence Wigmore and his newlywed wife, Peg (Jenkins) Wigmore, had a new house built on Alden Avenue. Lawrence worked for PSE&G

and Peg was a school teacher. She played basketball during her college days with the first all girls basketball team at Glassboro College in about 1928-1930. Oh yes! Miss Peggy Jenkins was one of our forerunners, not only shooting hoops but also shooting at that GLASS ceiling. Peg graduated from Palmyra High School. She lettered in basketball and hockey and is also a member of the Palmyra High School, "Hall of Fame." She gave up teaching after her first born arrived. Peg and Lawrence raised four daughters and one son. The first born was Peggy, and then Lorraine, Ginny, Marilyn, and Larry.

They lived four houses from us and they were very neighborly. My two brothers, being much younger than I, attended school with the Wigmore children as they were all close in age. Their mother, being a school teacher, was very strict with them. Always making sure they finished their homework right after school. It was no surprise to me in later years, seeing Lorraine's name on a ballot running for Mayor of Delran. She married Lenard Schmeirer at the time; he was another musician here in town and was great with the Trumpet. Lorraine served as Mayor from 1972 to 1984. She also served as the president for the Council of Mayors for the state of New Jersey and was the first elected Mayor of Delran Wow! Look who also took a shot at that GLASS ceiling, we were so proud of her here in "The Park." Until 1972 all previous mayors were chosen by the township committee, yes in 1972 Delran became a democracy and Lorraine also held office during Delran's 100th Anniversary in 1980.

Lorraine fought tooth and nail for our war veterans. There was a time when the veteran's administration wanted to take Ed Lipinsky's disability pension away just because he was operating a small service station to supplement his income; well, they bumped into the wrong person when they took on Lorraine. She made sure that Ed Lipinsky continued to receive his Veterans disability check. She also made sure that Frank Tighe was hired for the public works department, (Frank was a prisoner of war and when he came home he was in need of a job, he suffered from post traumatic stress disorder). He was grateful for the job and never made Lorraine sorry that she hired him; he worked hard every day he was there.

George Baker and his wife were the old fashion type people that stayed around home. If Mrs. Baker answered the door, she would always be wearing an apron as this was her badge of honor, signifying that she was a house wife, and home maker. George worked as a machinist at the Keystone Watch Case in Riverside. They had a son, George Jr., and a daughter, Rose.

I worked at the Keystone with George for two years and when his daughter, Rose, was about to get married George asked if I could supply the music. He knew I would say yes. After all, we were neighbors. My sister Eleanore and Rose were good friends at the time and Eleanore knew the husband to be, Tom Adams, who later became Chief of Police in Cinnaminson.

The wedding reception was held in Bakers back yard on a beautiful June afternoon, and there were streamers looped from tree to tree and the food was some of Mrs. Baker's fine recipes. We played music, that is, Harry, John and I, for a good three hours or more. Rosie Baker was as pretty as a rose and Tom was very tall and handsome. They had a happy life together and we as neighbors were happy for them.

Charlie Cotton and his son, Bob, lived in two bungalows side by side, Bob's sister, Rebecca, lived with her father Charlie. It seemed their mother had passed away some years before we knew them. Bob was working and raising a young family. Charlie was retired at the time, so while my father was building our first house on Alden Ave. and only a building lot between the Cottons' and our house, my father and Charlie became good friends. While we were building the house, Charlie would come over and lend a hand whenever he could.

When our house was finished my father went out and bought a new 1941 ford sedan. Then one day while he and my mother went shopping, my sister decided to cook. Well it didn't take long before she had the kitchen on fire, the flames were licking up the wall behind the stove and the smoke drove all of us out of the house.

Fortunately, the kitchen door was on the side toward the Cottons house and Charlie, seeing all the commotion and being a fireman and a farmer, grabbed the best tool he had, and ran straight to the open kitchen door and with his shovel in hand, began throwing sand from the side yard onto the stove. Well to our amazement the fire was out before the fire truck got there, but for safety sake the fireman added a little water to the stove and wall. When our parents came home they were shocked to see the mess, but then happy to see we kids were fine. My father couldn't thank Charlie enough, after that episode we became close friends with the Cotton family.

Charlie's son, Bob, and I have been lifelong friends and worked on cars together at the house. After they purchased the farm in back of Dennelers coal yard, Bob and his family moved out to the old farmhouse. I did visit them at the time, but then as time went by we were both busy with our families. Then one day a knock on the door and wouldn't you know, it was my old friend Bob Cotton, we had many long conversations after that. I do see his son Lester at the American Legion when I get there.

Our neighbor, Lawrence Haines, had a nickname Hooley, and he would never admit to the name Lawrence. Anyway Hooley was always active in the community and in 1938 he got a few guys together and carved out a piece of ground over on the left-hand side of Norman Ave. close to Lake St. This was the perfect place for sand lot baseball.

Hooley collected up as much equipment as he could. Some of the boys had gloves and bats, and with a make shift back stop and a wooden bench we were in business. John Smith and I were left fielders. He would start and play two innings and then hand the glove to me for two innings, then he would play the last two innings and the game was over. The reason he let me use his glove was to convince me that I could play baseball, but that never happened, sports was not my bag.

Hooley would split the boys up into two teams and do the best he could to teach the boys that good old American game of Baseball. Hooley was an auto mechanic and a chauffeur for business men around town, Joe Raphael gave Hooley his start as a chauffeur and I don't think Joe ever drove after that. Hooley was active with the Park Fire Company and his wife, Marian, belonged to the Ladies Auxiliary.

The next two houses #26 and #28 Alden were built by my father,

Francis Klingler. When #28 was finished my father sold #26 to my sister Shirley, and her husband, Bill Steedle. My sister, Eleanore, and her husband bought a home on Chester Ave. When I came home from the service there were five of us living at #28 Alden, my father, my mother, Helen, my two brothers, Francis and Wayne, and myself.

When we lived at #26 my father had a small machine shop in the back yard about 30ft. from the house. When we moved to #28 all the tools and machines were moved with us. The basement was large enough for a small machine shop, an optical shop and a bench dedicated for cutting and polishing stones. At the front of the basement we had a regulation size pool table.

My father had everything he needed to keep us three boys busy. He had more ambition then anyone I ever knew, he was contently teaching. He played violin and piano and so my two brothers and I became musicians. We had to play chess in the winter and pool after dinner. When we went down to the basement there was a sign hung from the bottom rafter with two words,

"The'La'Bor'atory" this is where we were taught the fine art of machine work, and I must mention optics.

We built a six inch reflector telescope; the six inch mirror was ground and polished in the optical shop. The hardware was made in the machine shop. Plus the testing equipment that tested for spherical aberrations in the parabolic surface of the mirror. This telescope was setup in the backyard about 10 o'clock at night. The first thing we focused on was the moon, and that was great, but then we swung the telescope around to the west and there it was. We could actually see the rings around Saturn.

When my sister Shirley, and her husband, Bill Steedle, lived next door, the two granddaughters, Terrie and Donna, were at our house quite often. Terrie was an animal lover like her father, Bill. He raised boxer dogs for a time, and then bought a race horse and a show horse for Terrie. She rode in competitions and did very well; Terrie still works with animals as I write.

Donna Steedle, who attended Rider College in Lawrenceville, N.J., needed a project for one of her college courses. She had a scientific journal about photographing (Beta wave particles) and asked my father and me to look it over while she went back to college. The first thing we did was to make a list of things we had and the things we needed. Well the list of things we needed was fairly large, but we knew the project was feasible.

So we rolled up our sleeves, and after a few weeks we were building the instrumentation to photograph Beta wave particles. When Donna came home from college she would always come to the shop and check out this project of hers. My father would teach her and let her make parts. The one thing she liked and learned to do, was to drill holes in glass jars, she also helped making small brackets. By the time the project was finished she knew every part and piece and their purpose, she also had the expertise to head up the project.

There were electrical and electronic circuits to test, vacuums on glass containers, camera shutter timing and lighting. We tested everything without the radioactive material. Then we let Donna decide the next step. These were the choices; we could get a small sample of radioactive material from the Franklin Institute. Or, Donna could take the project back to college with her, where they could supply the material. This is exactly what she did. By the way, certain radioactive materials radiate particles of different kinds at different rates. This is known as decay, we were only concerned with materials that exhibited "Beta wave particles".

I have to apologize for all this technical babble, so! Here is the simple explanation. An apple falls from a tree and hits the ground. Now as the apple "decays" it disintegrates leaving all of its energy into the atmosphere and into the ground. An isotope like Potassium 40 is a good example; as it decays it radiates "Beta wave particles" into the atmosphere. These are the particles she had to photograph. When Donnas' photographs were compared with the samples the College had, they were very much the same. She won a scholarship award and donated all the equipment to Rider College. Then went on to work for MacMillan & Collier, where she was Vice President of the children's book Department.

We not only went to school during the day, we were also home schooled at night and weekends. As I write, my brother, Wayne, is a director of a ten piece dance band in New Hampshire and brother, Francis, has a wood working shop where he makes fine cabinetry and custom made pool cues. Well, that's enough about the family. After all there were people in this community with talents you wouldn't believe.

Margret Maguire lived across the street and next to the Pond. This was a good size lot, it was about 60ft. wide and 225ft. deep and there was enough ground between our house and Margret's to build another house. Somewhere in the late 50's the township cut a road through here and named it Burge.St. Margret lived here with her daughter Peggy and when Peggy married John Russik, they moved to a new house in Riverside. Margret sold the house to the Avery family. Bill Avery worked in maintenance for the Zurbrugg Hospital in Riverside. When Bill found out that I refereed wrestling matches for the Riverside Turners wrestling team, he hardly missed a match. He and many others like him, helped to support these wrestling events that raised funds for organizations here in town.

Mr. & Mrs. George Lane and their daughter June, lived across the street on the corner of Alden & Lake St. Mrs. Lane had a beautiful parrot that had all the colors of the rainbow. In the summer she kept this large parrot in a birdcage by the side window. This bird loved to talk to people as they walked by. George was a machine shop Foreman at the Keystone Watch Co. in Riverside. In 1950 I worked for George before I became a tool and die maker. He and I became very good friends over the years.

Now let me tell you about Folz's Pond. Home is where the heart lies, but it's also a place with deep seated memories that linger on through the years. Oh yes, the memories of our youthful days especially those days at Folz's Pond. Like the words from fiddler on the roof, "those were the days my friends we thought they'd never end." Everyone who grew up in "The Park" remembers those cold winter days and nights when the pond became frozen over like a sheet of glass. We boys had to test our skills at building bond fires and stepping out on the ice to make sure it was safe for skating. We were always looking around to see if the girls were watching. They were probably thinking; look at those dummies walking out on that ice!

But we were here to skate, and skating we did, as long as it was safe. One of our favorite ploys was the whip. It consisted of a line of boys all holding hands, with one in the center of the pond known as the pivot. As this line started to skate around in a circle, the boys closest to the pivot would pick up speed. This would create a whip and the boy on the end would soon fly off across the ice and stumble onto the bank, and yes there was always that unsuspected girl, who found her way to the end of this line, not knowing that she was about to become the brunt of this joke and wind up rolling across the ice and onto the bank. No one ever got injured-after all; we were wrapped from head to toe in winter clothes.

There were times when someone would fall through the ice, oh yes the night John Smith, Freddie Myers and I fell through the ice. We were up to our chest in water that was about the deepest part of the Pond. My house was the second house from the pond and so we made our way through Maguire's back yard over to my back porch. When I opened the back door my father took one look, and motioned us to come in and get close to the wood burning cast iron stove.

He wrapped towels around us while my mother made hot chocolate, after the warmth of the wood stove and the hot chocolate, our muscles started to relax and all that shivering stopped. It was time to laugh but not to forget that cold icy water. Many years later Fred Myers would talk about the hot chocolate and the wood stove and my father's concern when he saw us dripping wet at the back door.

By the way, that small shop is where I sharpened ice skates for .25 cents that was about minimum wage at the time. When I talked about writing this book, all of my friends would say, don't forget those days at Folzies Pond, yes we added a couple letters to the name so it became "Folzie's pond or just the Pond."

Now let me tell you about my experience living close to the pond during spring and summer months. There were goldfish and turtles in this pond and during the winter the goldfish were frozen in the ice, they must go into a type of hibernation.

In the spring they would thaw out, and then you could watch them swim close to the bank. There are little tadpoles and frogs but the best of all is at night, with the screens in place and the windows open all the little frogs and katydids come out to sing a night time lullaby. This is the true meaning of tranquility, even to this day living one street over from the pond, on a warm summer's night; I can hear this night time symphony that fills my heart and soul with good memories that lulls me to a profound sleep. I wish everyone could experience one night near Folzies pond.

The Lipinsky's lived on the opposite side of the pond. There was Walter Lipinsky and his wife, Charlotte, with six children Margret, Bill, Ed, Gertrude and Ruth. They also had a son, Walter, who left us too early in life. Their oldest daughter, Margret, married Frederick Toffel, who we mentioned before living on Chester Ave. their son Bill made his home next to Folz Pond, the younger three Ed, Gert, and Ruth lived home in the early 40's. Walter, whom we only knew as Mr. Lipinsky, worked as a Chemist for U.S. Pipe, Fleetwings in Bristol, and Beaunit Mills in Beverly.

At home he kept quite busy with his house and property which extended over to Stewart Ave. He was seen many times coming up Stewart Ave. from the river with a wheelbarrow piled high with driftwood, which he chose carefully. He would wheel the wood through the back of his lot at Stewart, over to Alden where he cut and stacked it in a neat pile.

Every spring he would work on his garden, and I must say, a very large and well kept garden. He and his two sons would turn the soil over by hand, this was hard work. They each had a spade type shovel that was pushed into the ground with their foot, lifted it up and turn it over, and then they would backup one step and repeat this process over and over. I can't recall how many rows they turned over, but it seems to me that garden was 50 by 100 ft. or more. No wonder these two boys grew up to be 6ft. tall with broad shoulders and mussels to spare. The back part of this property went all the way over to Stewart Ave. and was later donated to the township for Friendship Park. There are basketball court, swings, benches, and the assorted playground equipment for the little tike, and is well kept.

Mrs. Lipinsky like many other house wives knew how to preserve these vegetables from the garden. She not only stored and preserved food, but also prepared food for her family and others. She was the head cook for the cafeteria at Cambridge Elementary School for 35 years. This family had all the attributes from Europe and their parents before them, they were God fearing, down to earth type people that knew the real value of life, and practiced this every day.

I always marveled at Bill Lipinsky, he worked full time for the Riverside Post Office, and served a number of years as Postmaster, but his dedication to the Park Community Church was something I noticed over the years. His wife Ethel, and their daughters, served as his backup when he was in need of Sunday School Teachers. In his spare time he was studying theology, and on Sunday he gave sermons at the Church.

During the week he would cut the grass, trim the bushes and limbs from the trees, and it seemed like there was always some type of maintenance that had to be taken care of. Bill was always there making sure these things got done. I'd say he had the patience of Job. One by one he introduced his siblings to the Church and they became life time members. Even as I write, this family is still doing their part in keeping this Church open on Sunday. Not to say there were no struggles along the way. In 1928 Walter and Charlotte lost their eight year old son, Walter Jr., who was a drowning victim during a day at Clementon Amusement Park.

Then came the "War Years." America was trying to stay neutral as the war was getting worse in Europe, but then came the attack on Pearl Harbor, which was shocking to everyone. The day after the attack President Roosevelt declared war on Germany and Japan. Before the draft by lottery was set up and running, young boys were enlisting by the hundreds, Bill enlisted in the U.S. Army, and not too long after Ed (Pinky) Lipinsky enlisted in the U.S. Marine Corp. most of the people here in "The Park" only knew Ed by his nick name, and that was Pinky

Lipinsky. You can see where the nick name came from, if you take the pin-ky from Lipinsky.

Finky was a six foot broad shouldered kind hearted man, with a wonderful outlook on life, but now everything has changed. The nick name was gone and Ed Lipinsky was part of the U.S. Marine Corp. and his older brother, Bill Lipinsky, in the U.S. Army. It was heart wrenching for the parents, but they knew their boys wanted to fulfill their duties and serve this great country. It seemed like a long time that they were gone, but after basic training they both came home before shipping out. Naturally there had to be some sibling rivalry between these two boys who had just turned into men. Yes they both declared that their branch of service was the best, but the argument turned into a stalemate, so they shock hands and wished each other the best.

Bill was shipped to Europe and Ed was shipped to the Pacific. Ed was in the Battle of Iwo Jima on February 19, 1945 this is a small Island about 600 miles south of Tokyo, Japan. His company of Marines stormed the beach under extreme resistant's from Japans forces which were heavily fortified in bunkers. Unfortunately Ed was severely wounded and left for dead along the beach with hundreds of his comrades. Four days after the invasion Ed was found, miraculously on top of a death pile of men, still breathing.

He was patched up and brought back to the States where he spent almost two years at the Naval Hospital in Newport, Road Island. When his doctor was transferred to Bethesda Naval Hospital in Maryland, they also transferred Ed so his doctor could follow up with his treatment. The doctor also wrote a personal letter to Ed's parents saying how Ed was determined to get back on his feet. On his first trip home he was met at the 30th Street Station by Joe Raphael and a school bus filled with friends and school mates that were there to bring him home, what a joyous occasion.

This was a little before I came home from the service, but when I did, I had to meet with Ed. I knew he was very independent but as a close friend and neighbor I had to know the extent of his injuries. He said that most of his injuries were on his right side, and that he had metal plates, screws and wires, from his foot all the way up to his shoulder that held his bones together.

When he first came home he would force himself to walk every day, and his favorite path was through the back yard, over to Stewart Ave. and up to the main street to meet with friends and then walk back home. He favored his right leg quite a bit and in the early days he would stumble and fall, but he refused help getting up. I'm sure he didn't want anyone pulling on his arms, after all, his ribs were wired together plus the plates and screws in his arms and legs were fragile, and after two years in the Naval Hospital he knew how to handle himself.

As time went on he became stronger and went on to get married at the Park Community Church to his lovely wife Lillian, whom he met at the Delrando Diner. They bought a house across Fairview St. and Rt. 130 and opened a small Gas Station, raised two sons and two daughters and in 1962 he became Mayor of Delran. A sad note, his father passed away a few months before Ed became Mayor. His father would've been so proud of him. This was a typical family during the war years and beyond, they were determined to stay close together with God's blessings. One note, I don't believe Ed Lipinsky ever knew that the U.S.S. Melvin DD680 a Destroyer with S 1/c Ed (eggie) Horton aboard were supporting air cover for the U.S. Marines landing on Iwo Jima.

Otto and Hilda Grockenberger were both born around the French and German border in Europe. They came to America in the early 1900's. They met by chance at the Lutheran Church in Riverside, a German speaking town with Factories, Churches, Schools and Social Clubs. Hilda was sponsored by her Aunt Helen Daehne who owned a maternity house in Riverside. She wanted Hilda to become a Nurse and brought her here. Otto was a builder by trade, and came to this country by route of his uncle's farm in Pennsylvania, and then to Riverside.

It didn't take long for Otto to find work in this town. Soon he and Hilda met at one of the town's functions and began to date, and then in 1926 they were married at the Lutheran Church in Riverside. Now, Otto wanted to be part of the community so the first thing he did was to help with the building of the Riverside Tuners hall. When the building was finished, and he wanted to become a member, they informed him that he had to become a naturalized citizen. As soon as Otto received his citizenship papers; he applied and became a member of the Turner Organization.

After a few years Otto and Hilda moved to Riverside Park where they rented a house on Alden Avenue and began raising a family. As the family became too large for this house, Otto purchased a large piece of ground and built a beautiful home on the other side of the street. As time went on, he built a house for Walter and Jean Ester was already married with her own home. That left Betty and Richard at home. Then Walter tried to enlist in the U.S. Navy and was rejected, he was only 16 years of age.

In 1944 he enlisted in the Merchant Marines, oh yes during the Second World War the Merchant Marines were taking young boys at the age of 16. Walt Otto Grockenberger boarded a ship at New York and set sail across the ocean. This was the beginning of many trips to places like Italy, Japan, Panama, Okinawa, the Philippines, the Dutch West Indies and places I haven't documented. The Government didn't recognize the Merchant Marines as part of the armed services, but like Walt said, "without them we couldn't have continued to press on with the war." The Merchant Marines died at a rate that proportionately exceeded all other military branches except the Marine Corps.

When the war ended Walt returned home to Riverside Park, however he didn't stray too far from the water. For the next four years he served in the U.S. Coast Guard throughout the tri-state area. In 1949 Walt married Adele, the two met while he was stationed on Fisher's Island, NY.

When he retired from the Coast Guard he worked as a maintenance man for a few companies before taking a job as a custodian at Southern Regional High School, while he lived in Barnegat in 1969. He also helped found the Pinewood Estates Volunteer Fire Company.

He was a community minded person and loved his country and always said he was hopeful that the wave of patriotism in America continues on. One thing he said he will always remember from his time on the tanker was returning to New York harbor at the end of the war and seeing the Statue of Liberty. There was not a prettier sight in the world than that lady welcoming us back home.

While living in Barnegat Walt's nephew, George Kenny, Sr., past Commander of the American Legion Post 115 Beverly City had discovered the awards his uncle Walter qualified for while researching military records. Walt was highly honored for his service to his country; he was one of only 10 merchant marines that sailed in all three theaters of the war, the Mediterranean, the Atlantic and the Pacific War Zones and has received all three Medals and bars plus the Distinguished Service Medal, and the World War II Victory Medal for his service in the Merchant Marines during the War.

John & Myrtle Smith lived across the street from the Volkman's. They had quite a large family, 7 boys and 6 girls., From the youngest to the oldest there was Myrtle, John Jr. Charlie, Eleanor, Eddie, Helen, Betty, Phillip, Leon, Billy, Harry, Kathy, and Judy. Over the years Mrs. Smith lost 6 children, some from miscarriages and others who passed away at an early age, the number of children has always been a controversy over the years, but I'm sure 19 is the right number.

When I was 11 years old we moved from Stewart Ave. to Alden. John and I became very close friends. I can still remember how proud he was of his name, John Wesley Smith Jr. I've seen him write this on many papers. I guess our friendship started for the fact that we lived on the same street, went to the same school and both played music. John played Accordion and I Guitar, I just can't tell you how many hours we spent together playing music.

I have a picture on the wall, just above my computer desk of Harry Stevenson on drums, myself on guitar, John on accordion, with his brother Charlie on guitar. This was the first group that John got together. He was our booking manager from the first day till the last. As a sideline, John and his brother, Billy, I and my two brothers, Fran and Wayne, were members of the Riverside String band for quite a few years. Our four piece dance band turned into a three piece band when Charlie gave up playing. He had heart problems and passed away at a young age.

The three of us continued to play music for weddings and social and holiday dances. I remember sitting at the same table with the Smith family and eating with them. Mrs. Smith would cook a meal in one large pot, set it in the middle of the table, feed the little one's first and then the rest of the kids including John and I. I'm not too sure how she did it, but she sure could cook up a good meal in that big pot.

Naturally I became close with John's mother and father and his sisters and brothers over the years. It's something to see a family get along so well, they just seem to have so much respect for one another. Every once in a while I meet up with one or two of those who are still living, and they always greet me like I'm one of the family. If you don't think I have tears in my eyes while I'm writing this, think again.

There were five families, the Volkmans, Shnecher, Kelvey's Sundermiers, and Bowkers who lived down here at the end of Alden Ave. For a short time that is in the early years when the banks of the Delaware River and the Rancocus Creek were very low, every time the moon was full and the tide was high, these families' yards were flooded. Then in the 60's the county built the river bank about four feet higher, with the exception of Stewart Ave. At this very spot the storm sewer pipe has been compromised and in recent years with the water table rising there's flooding again.

Part 13

Norman Ave.

Raymond Hammel, his wife Mildred, and two children Elaine and Raymond Jr. lived in the first house. Ray was a carpenter and one of the last houses he built was Charlie Shinns house on St. Mihiel Drive. Elaine and her brother, Ray, attended Cambridge School. They lived here just a short while and then moved to Florida. It seems funny how some people can up and move and never come back, and others live here for a lifetime.

Morrison Fields, his wife and children lived on the other side of the street. There was one more house next to them and nothing else on this side but a wooded area all the way down to the old Mansion. Morrison attended Cambridge School and whenever the teacher left the room, Morrison would be staring out the window and dreaming of things nearer his heart, which could have been anything but the latest assignment for that school day. He was only a few years out of school when he married and started a family. Later he was diagnosed with asthma, and moved to the shore where he spent his last days. I don't think the salt air really helped. My Uncle Albert who lived here in "The Park" also had asthma. His doctor told him to move west, so he packed up and moved to Denver Colorado where he found a job at the Gates Rubber Plant. After a short time his symptoms went away. He married, had children and lived in Denver the rest of his life.

Ed Reeves built his home next to Hammel's. Ed married my mother's first cousin, Anna. They had one daughter, Charlotte. Ed was in the excavating business. He had a front end loader and two trucks and lived there about ten years and then sold the house to Dick & Ruth Gilbert. Dick wasn't here long before he joined the Fire Co. He went on to become supervisor of the Streets Department here in Delran.

There was a large lot and a tennis court that belonged to Charlie Springer. This was a regulation size court with a clay surface. This family loved tennis. Charlie and his wife raised two sons, Henry and John. Charlie Springer invested in real-estate and building lots. He seemed to be very reserved. The boys went to St Pete's school in Riverside. I guess that's why I never got to know them. One summer day the fire siren sounded and we noticed the fire truck going down Norman Ave. towing the rescue boat, I knew what that meant so I ran over to Lake Street and saw the firemen putting the boat in the water. It wasn't long before they pulled a young lifeless boy from the water, it was Henry Springer. They lived one block from where Henry drowned. I'll never forget his mother with tears rolling down her cheeks as she held her hands to her face. When you live close to Lakes and Rivers there's always boating and drowning accidents. It wasn't long before the Springer family moved away.

This house was later sold to Charlie and Ruth Ercol. They had two sons, Chuck and Guy and a daughter, Darleen, Charlie was the superintendent at Lakeview Memorial Park and as a side line he opened up a Bait and Tackle Shop at his home, and soon got the name Cap Ercol. He kept this business going after he retired from Lakeview. Over the years Cap Ercol's business is and was, mostly with Riverside Marina and Dredge Harbor Yacht Basin, Cap has a great personality, and is liked by the fishermen in this area. His business has grown over the years.

Well Charlie Cap Ercol has left us at the age of 86. He was a Veteran of the Second World War and the Korean War, a member of the VFW post 3020, a former chief of the Delran Emergency Squad and a past president of the Delran Fire Co. What a busy man. He was one of those good looking and good mannered guys that everyone enjoyed. Ruth (Smith) Ercol was raised next door, her parent's house set back about 40 feet giving them a nice size front yard. She has a sister Shirley Davenport over on Alden Ave. and a brother Bud Smith on Chester Ave. and a brother Joe who is deceased. They were all raised here and probably born here and stayed here because they love it here. Once you get Riverside Park in your blood you never get it out. By the way! There were three families of Smith's here at one time, and none of them were related.

Ray Jauss and his wife Ruth moved here from Philadelphia in the mid 40's. They had a daughter named Faith who was a victim of Polio at a young age. They made many trips to one of the Philadelphia Hospitals. After time they had to fit her with leg braces. Ruth was a house wife and a good musician. She played piano and wrote many songs. There was at that time a company in New York City that bought music and lyrics. If they accepted your song they would send you a check for fifty dollars. Ruth sold quite a few songs in those early days. Ray played alto saxophone and banjo. His brother, Russ, played sax with the Ferko string band. Once in a while Russ who lived in Philly would come over to Rays' for a jam session. I played guitar and had fun jamming with them. As soon as Ray moved here he joined the Fire Company and served as Recording Secretary and was part of the "Committee of Nine" which was the beginning of the Emergency Squad. He was a dedicated member for a lifetime.

Ray was employed at the Philadelphia Navy Yard as a communication specialist. He would test telephone systems throughout the ship. At home he had a radio room and his FCC Amateur Radio License. Most people in the neighborhood would see Ray pushing his little daughter faith up and down the sidewalk on a three wheel bike, she couldn't walk at the time and with special pedals and Ray pushing she got her leg exercise.

Faith grew up, married and raised two daughters. Ruth and Ray lived in this house until the day they left us, they were my friends forever. Every once in awhile I sit down at the piano and play one of the songs Ruth taught me, it seems like she's still looking over my shoulder.

There was one more house here on the corner of Lake St. which was a rental; people were in and out for years. Norman and Shirley Davenport's daughter, Dawn, and husband bought this house and have lived here for years. Dawn has served as a crossing guard at Chester Ave. middle School for many years. There were only houses on the corners of Lake St.

On the next corner lived the Andersons. Lewis Sr. his wife, three daughters, Helen, Mildred, Pearl, and a son, Lewie Jr. They had a half acre of ground with the house located on the far side of the property. Lew Sr. operated a trucking business from this address he had two tanker trucks which he and his son-in-law, Al Latwinas, hauled fuel oil. He also had two stock cars which he raced at Arnies Mount and Atco race track. His son-in-law, Al, drove #27 and George Fields drove #27 Jr. and I served as their machinist/mechanic. It was a lot of fun but also a lot of work.

Sometimes when we got back early from the race track, Mrs. Anderson would have soda and snacks in the kitchen and sometimes Lew Sr. would bring out his five string banjo and entertain us. He could play and sing and perform tricks like swinging the banjo back and forth, spinning it around in a ring and all the time singing laughing and never missing a beat. I'll tell you that man was a piece of work.

His, son, Lewie, had a birth defect which I talked about earlier and now I'd like to tell the real story that very few people know, at home lewie would jump into his father's car and drive it around the back yard. It was a 1938 Ford with a stick shift and a clutch paddle on the floor. There were no automatic transmissions back then. It wasn't easy learning to drive but Lewie was persistent. One day he was at Raphaels garage and Joe said his driver hadn't showed up and Lewie said, "where do you want to go?", Joe said, "What do you mean?," Lewie said, "I can drive!," Joe looked at him in disbelief but Lewie insisted, so Joe got in his car with Lewie in the driver's seat. They went down Stewart Ave., around the block and back up to River Road and turned in Stewart Ave. and parked. Joe got out of the car and walked back to his office shaking his head.

On the way around the block Lewie asked Joe if he would help him get his driver's license. This is something I didn't know at the time, but now I know why Joe was shaking his head. He told Lewie he would think about it. In the meantime Joe made some phone calls and got the support he needed. The first one he called was Bill Gould. He was a

Motor Vehicle Inspector. Between the two of them they came up with a plan. Joe drove Lewie to the motor vehicle station in Burlington where they met Bill Gould. Lewie took the test, answered all the questions, and was told that he would have to modify his car and come back and have it checked out.

This is when I got involved without knowing it. I had been working as an apprentice machinist in the family machine shop for my Uncle Paul and my father. Joe Raphael called my uncle and told him the situation and the next thing I knew, I was machining all the parts for Lewie's car and this wasn't the end. Later on Joe had called up Joe Denneler and asked him if he needed a driver. I don't know what was said, but again I was making special parts for a coal truck.

Later when I was at Dennelers installing the parts on the truck, Joe Denneler asked me if I would ride the coal truck with Lewie for a few days. I told him that I'd have to ask my father and my uncle first. Joe said that's all taken care of it's up to you. The few days turned into two weeks plus and I liked helping Lewie out but I wanted to get back to my trade so Joe got another volunteer from "The Park" namely Marvin Heck. Later on Lewie's father purchased a dump truck and put Lewie to work hauling sand and gravel, and again I took care of the modifications.

Lewie was one of the best drivers I ever knew. He showed his appreciation to everyone by driving (40) forty years without an accident and on his fortieth year his insurance co. held a party and presented Lewie with a plaque and a certificate at the Riverside Park Fire house.

John Wigmore had a nice business here at Norman Ave. His backyard was quite deep and filled with Azalea Plants. This was the beginning of "Wigmore Nursery." During the summer when school was out John would hire kids from the neighborhood to plant Azalea shoots in two feet square flat boxes packed with two inches of very dark rich soil. He had these flat wooden boards with small nail spaced 1 inch apart protruding through one side. Our job was to take this board with all the nails and place it on top of that two feet flat box, push down and then pull back up carefully. This would leave a lot of holes in the soil, and then the process was to place one Azalea shoot in each hole. John would pay us for each flat we finished. You didn't have to be a speed demon to make money here; you just had to do a good job.

After a few years John moved to Moorestown at the corner of Bridgeboro & Haines Mill Rd. This gave him more acreage for his business. I knew John very well, and knew how to get along with him. He didn't realize that I had sympathy for him, and if he did he would have fired me in a minute. My father taught me to have sympathy for the misfortunate and when I first met Lewie Anderson I remembered what my father had tough me. These people didn't want sympathy they wanted respect.

We've come along a rough and tough road over the years. I remember the things people said about the handicap and the nick names they had to put up with. Harry Stevenson had Polio as a kid, his nick name was "Polely." It took a few years for him to shed that name. Harry and Lewie never complained what fate had handed them. They were the greatest guys to get along with. I knew John Wigmore was bitter deep inside and sometimes his anger would show through, but believe me I have seen his good side from time to time. These Polio victims suffered with pain and never said a word about it. In time, with exercise the pain was reduced and braces were removed. What I didn't know was that in later life the pain returns. What fortitude!

Tom Vathis and his wife, Ida, bought their house in 1969 Tom and Ida still live here as I write. Their children are all grown up and living in Riverside, Delran and Somerdale. They have three daughters and one son. Tom has worked as an Auto and Diesel mechanic all his life. He's happily retired now and his wife, Ida, is also retired from driving school bus in Riverside for 27 years. She seemed to be a natural at the job, the kids all loved her. I know this first hand, for the fact that my two grandsons, Tim and Mike Wasco, road this bus to baseball games,

My daughter, Cindy, and Ida are good friends. They spent a lot of time with the Riverside boy's baseball team. Tom and Ida are well liked around town. They're so outgoing and a pleasure to be with. I'm sure you've met people like this before. They have seven grandchildren ranging from eighteen to six, and naturally they have become built in baby sitters, and I know they love it, "I hope they never move away".

Mrs. George Fields lived in the last house on Norman Ave. She had two sons, George and Morrison. Her first husband lost his life while working on the Tacony Palmyra Bridge. After a few years she married Jake Everham who had three daughters, Ernestine, Shirley and Dorothy. Now the Late Mrs. Fields became Mrs.Everham (nee) Doxey. She is also the sister of Mrs. John Smith (nee) Doxey of Alden Ave.

In the summer when we were young, we had block parties at the end of Norman and Alden Ave. The neighbors would get to gether with food and drink. John Smith and I would supply the music and everyone would sing and dance and have a good time. We boys liked to tease Mrs. Everham until she came out of the house with a broom. Then we had to run for cover. Once in a while she would catch up to one of us and swat us that broom.

I remember the time Toby Mosteller kept zig zagging in front of her and teasing her until he made the wrong move and she wacked him a good shot with that broom. You could see the surprise on his face. Well we all got a good laugh that day and every time the subject comes up we still get a good laugh from the look on Toby's face. It was all in good fun. I can still remember some of the cousins from John Smith's side of the family being there, some of the neighbors from Alden Ave. the Grokenbergers, the Myers Family and a few others from "The Park".

On the Westside of Norman Ave. there was a large Mansion. It was a home for orphan children and operated by a woman known as Aunt Mattie. There were some who were handicapped, especially the two children I remember. A little girl with no legs who had to crawl around to get anywhere, she died at a young age when her heart gave out. Then there was a boy who was placed outside in the summer, he would be tied to a chair so he could look out over the river where an occasional boat or ship would go by. He was totally retarded and the only thing he could do was make a strange growling sound. The neighbors felt sorry for Aunt Mattie and the children and would help when they could. In fact the

Everham family was the closest to the Mansion and many times Mrs. Everham would go and help Aunt Mattie feed the children.

It's sad to look back on some of these situations, but it also reminds us how good we have it. In time this home was closed and the building sat empty. A man by the name of Joe Reader bought quite a few acres of ground from Norman Ave. over to Dredge Harbor which included the old Mansion.

He was in the sand and gravel business dredging and shipping sand and gravel by barge over to Philadelphia. He started dredging where the old Dredge Harbor ended, which was about where the Custard stand is today. When he finished dredging the harbor came over to about 200 yard of Norman Avenue.

The VFW leased a portion of this property and the Mansion from Mr. Reader. They agreed to clean and paint inside and out and make all necessary repairs. They made a large picnic area and placed a sign at the front of the driveway with their name. (The VFW Post 3020 Delran). The whole project was finished right after the Second World War. They made a good size apartment on the second floor, where their custodian, Reds Townsend, and his family, lived for five years or more.

During the summer months they held picnics to raise money. There were lots of shade trees, picnic tables and benches and if I remember right, it was $3.00 for all the corn and hot dogs and beer you could eat and drink. In about twenty years time the VFW purchased ground on Fairview St in the Fairview section of Delran, built and moved into the new building in 1972. Joe Reader sold the business to the Amico Sand & Gravel Co. who demolished the old Mansion and was in the process of building Condo's on the water front but this didn't go over too well with the neighborhood. They claimed, that Norman Ave. would not be able to handle the traffic, and this was validated, so the County took over this property and turned it in to walking trails, and named it Amico Island Park. The Everham property and the house were demolished. There have been a lot of changes over the years.

After the Second World War, the boating industry started to flourish here in Riverside Park. The west side of Norman Avenue became Riverside Marina. Now let's not get confused with the name "Riverside". Many businesses in Delran used the name Riverside. You may remember Riverside Lanes bowling alley: Riverside Ford: Riverside Marina is definitely in the Riverside Park area of Delran. The boating industry grew rapidly in the 60's. That is when we lost our identity of 'Riverside Park" and became Delran. We still refer to this area as "The Park". Here are the names of the boating companies: Riverside Marina: Winter's Sail Center: Cherubini's Sail boats:

and along St. Mihiel Drive we have, Clarks Landing: Castle Harbor: Dredge Harbor Yacht.

This is the largest industry in Delran Township. How many boats are here in the Dredge Harbor Basin? About 1500 or more.

Yes, this is where Delran got its start, right here at a place known as Plum Point at the west end of Riverside Park, and the Delaware River next to Taylors Lane. Today this piece of land belongs to McCarter & Dallman.

This is my story about the place I hold close to my heart, and will always be known to me, and many others, as "The Park." I know you're well aware of this by now, but I also know as a historian of Delran, that I'd be remised by leaving out my brothers and sisters across the Railroad Tracks. So let's head south.

Part 14

Cambridge

Cambridge was always known as a Hamlet, with a population of about 350 people, with two ethnic backgrounds, Polish and Lithuanians. They were so much alike in their customs and their religion, that for years I considered them of one persuasion. They were very active in St, Casmir's Church in Riverside. I'm not too sure but I think the School and the Church were built around the turn of the century.

I went to school in Cambridge and it will always have a special place in my heart. Cambridge Elementary School had a diversity of children some Lithuanian, some Polish, some German and two families of blacks the Colman Twins and the Lindsey's, Buster, Susie, and David. We all seemed to get along together, and our differences, if any, didn't seem to matter.

Miss Elsie Bodine was the school principal, and no nonsense type teacher. Yes we complained about her then, but years later as we matured, there was nothing but praise for her. Here are some of the teachers I remember, Miss Mills, Mrs. Wolf, and our Music teacher Miss Wilson.

Sometime in the 1930's an auditorium was added to the back of the school, and whenever they had a stage play, John Smith and I would supply the music. The stage seemed to be about 20 feet wide. When the main curtain opened, you could see a doorway in the back. There were also doorways on each side. The doorways had purple plush curtain which matched the main curtain.

It seemed to me that the main caricature entered from the center back door and all the others entered from the side doors. I don't know about John, but I was so involved with the music that I could hardly keep up with the story line, it sure was a lot of fun.

We had volunteer mothers, who would come each day, and prepare lunch for us. One was Mrs. Breuer and the other was Mrs. Lipinsky. These lunches were exactly what they advocate today, they were mostly fresh salads and soups which we all enjoyed.

The school had a lot of improvements over the years. The county had to allocate funds for these schools and their projects, after all the tax revenues were small, and there were new schools being built as the population expanded.

When we left school at the end of the day, we always walked down Main Street. The house wives would be sitting on their front porches, keeping an eye on all the kids making sure they were getting home safe. When we got to the rail road crossing and River Road, Albert May was there to walk us across. He was not only the crossing guard, but also the custodian and maintenance man. He kept the furnace fired up in the cold winter months. It seemed like he was always there, as sure as night and day.

Once we got across the tracks, we headed along River Road and to our favorite short cuts on the way home. There were empty lots here and there. The first vacant lot started at Reserve Ave and the National Lock Washer Co. Foundation, which stuck up out of the ground a few inches. Once we crossed over that, we headed for Norman Ave. There were more lots here and there from Norman over to Alden, Stewart and Chester. These were the foot worn paths most of us followed, and naturally in small groups.

John Smith and I would always walk home together, and at times, Walt Grockenberger would be with us, then you would see Jack Esworthy, Norma Clarkson, and Jack Nauss walking together, They lived close to each other on Stewart Ave. Going to school was a different story. Each kid had his or her own pace. Some got up and out of the house on time and some a little later. There was always someone running to catch up with a friend, usually a boy, and the girls were always on time, but never the less, the routine hardly changed.

Here's a sad story. I would leave Alden Ave. take my usual short cut over to Norman Ave. and wait for Mahlon Wicks and John Smith to catch up. This one morning John and I waited as long as we could, and then finally left without Mahlon. Later that day while in school, the teacher made an announcement to the affect that Mahlon Wicks had accidentally drowned. "What a punch in the stomach". It's hard to describe all the thoughts that go around in your head. Now I understand why schools bring in counselors as soon as possible. Back then, the word counselor wasn't in our vocabulary. Many times over the years when there was a drowning, I would think of Mahlon and that accident. Oh well, enough about that.

Cambridge was three square blocks starting at Front St. along the Rail Road over to Arch, then 2nd, 3rd, and 4th Street going south, then going east to Main, Chestnut and Brown. The School faced 3rd street. On the corner of 4th and Main was the Polish American Citizens Club (PACC) built in 1925, and is still open as I write. There were a few businesses here in Cambridge. The first two were on Chestnut Street, on the left hand side in between 2nd an 3$^{rd;}$ a butcher shop operated by Joe Astroski Sr. He came here from the old country, where he learned his trade, and kept this business going till the day he died. Down on the corner of 3rd and Chestnut across from the school there was a candy store owned by the Swadgeus family. The corner front door and steps are still visible today. On the corner of Front and Main there was a Pool Room owned and operated by Frank Yansic, who in later years became Mayor of Delran. On the other corner was a Grocery store, owned by the Johnson family. On the opposite side of Main St. Sam Zebrowski had a small Bar Room and a bottling plant, where he bottled Crescent Soda, his own brand. There was a Barber Shop on the left side of Main St. owned and operated by Mr. Ladzinski. After the Second World War, Chick Bauer opened a Dry Cleaning Store on 3rd. Street. Other than that there were two farms, one to the east side, which belonged to Andy Kentzinger, and one on the west side belonging to Charlie Harris.

There was an unofficial junk yard back in the woods, between Arch Street and the Harris farm. It belonged to a man known as Janowski, who lived in a shack, with his son, and daughter, and were dirt poor. Back in the early days of Delran, there were squatters, who lived on the land so long, that they had certain rights to that land until they died. One day Janowski and his kids just up and disappeared, no one knew what happened to them. In time the junk yard sunk into the ground and the old shack cough fire and burnt to the ground. This left the township with a mess to clean up. Years later this area became known as Lake Lonnie.

Joe Salkowski was the town plumber and worked out of a small truck. He lived on chestnut Street with his wife, and two daughters, Irene and Frances. He was a big guy and could crawl into tight places, that's the way most plumbing jobs were. Everyone liked Joe, a pleasant guy and a hard worker that always gave you a good job for your money. This little town was filled with so many nice people. They were like their parents before them, coming from the old county and appreciated everything they had.

Steve Kozianowski lived on the corner of Front and Chestnut Street, with his wife, and two children, Carroll and Marian. Steve worked at the Keystone Watch Co. and walked home for lunch every day weather permitting. He had a full head of wavy blond hair, and was the picture of health, no wonder he lived to be 90. His son Carroll, and I were classmates at Cambridge school. We are still good friends living in Delran. In the early days most of the people worked in the factories in Riverside, Later on they found work at Campbell's Soup, RCA Victor and Radio Condenser in Camden. N.J.

There were two families of Yoka's on Chestnut Street. The one I remember the most is Clem Yoka. He worked for RCA in Camden and had a great knowledge of electronics. His neighbors couldn't say enough good things about him. He was always ready to help someone especially if they had a radio that was acting up or a piece of electronic equipment that stopped working, that's when he would be there to help.

He was a soft spoken guy, tall and good looking but never flaunted these attributes. He found out from Ed Iwanicki, that I was also studying Electronics and the next time Clem and I met he wanted to convey all the fine points that I needed to know about Electronics, and how to make repairs. You just can't say enough about people who are there when you need them. There was another family of Yoka's Stanley, Edward, and their sister, Alfreda, and Holly Yoka, a cousin.

There were only a few houses on Brown St. and about the same, over to the west side of Arch St. and then a large farm belonging to the Sooy Family, which is now Lake Sooy. Then you come to Cambridge Woods, this is what they called the first woods which included the Race, Swedes Run, and the Harris farm.

Swedes Run is fed from the Delaware River through the Buck family farm, which is now Dredge Harbor, under River Road which is Buck's Bridge and then under the rail road and through the Harris farm and on out to Millside farm, then under Rt. 130 and keeps going over to Mooestown. The pool of water that we called the Race is part of Swedes Run.

I suspect the Harris family dug this watering hole for their live stock. They also built an all wood wagon bridge across this part of Swedes Run. I and many others stopped while crossing this bridge, just to watch the minnows and tadpoles swimming in this pool of crystal clear water.

I cannot remember a more serene place along Swedes Run, than this pool of water by the wagon bridge. It was a place where a person could take in the sweet smells, and the visual attributes of early spring, when the dogwood and honeysuckle were in bloom. Oh yes, there were more plants and arboretums to blossom, as summer strolled in.

When approaching the bridge, you may kick up a rabbit or two, and over head you may see a hawk or two as they glide gracefully just below those fluffy white clouds. Even those little finch and humming birds were flying from one place to another. It was like nature's time to show off her finest.

There were a few of us that liked this area for fishing. More than once we would meet up with Charlie Harris. We had a mutual respect for Charlie. If he was fishing at the Race, we would move downstream from him, he would speak to us as we walked by, just to let us know he acknowledged us. In earlier times, he let us know that we could fish here, as long as we stayed away from his house and barn. He was always the same and never changed, he was the last of the Harris family. This farm and this family date back to the 1700's.

In 1953 this area of the Harris farm became the famous Lake Lonnie and picnic grounds where people could bring their family to swim and picnic throughout the summer. People from north east Philly came over by the hundreds. It was a great escape from the boiling hot city.

This was the first woods and the only thing you could find here before Lake Lonnie was Indian artifacts. Many kids from the neighborhood would go to the second woods and find arrow heads. My young brother Wayne was always on the hunt for relics, he had a collection of arrow heads. When he was digging the foundation for his house, at the end of Arch St. and the second woods, he found some iron harness rings and bits from horses but also in the same dig, he found quite a few one inch iron shot or canon balls that could have came from the Revolutionary War. There was another story that lit my Brother Wayne's imagination which involved this Cambridge area of Swedes Run. This was about 1920 and the story goes like this. One evening our parents witnessed a ball of fire coming from the east and heading in the direction of Riverside, and continuing on down the railroad tracks toward Bucks Bridge near Swedes Run. It caused the lights in town to dim, and witnesses at the time said it had to be a Meteorite because of the loud sound that cracked some widows.

In the early 1950's Wayne was searching in this area with a metal detector when he came upon a strong signal. He began to dig and soon he had this grapefruit size object and knew right away, it was what he was looking for.

He had a small bench in the basement with a diamond cutting wheel and also some polishing equipment where he would cut and polish stones. He and my father sliced a sample piece off this object and mailed it to the Franklin Institute, where they confirmed it as a Meteorite.

He later moved to New Hampshire and took this funny looking

thing we called the moon rock with him. While digging over by Swedes Run, he found a utensil that looked like a pickle fork, the upper portion of the handle has the image of an Indian chief with full head dress, and could have been used as a trading piece.

On the east side of Brown Street, over to Chester Avenue, on Front Street, and all the way out to about 5th and Chester Ave. was Andy Kentzingers' farm. This was also considered part of Cambridge.

Some years back, there was a Railroad Crossing at Alden Avenue, when you crossed over to the other side, there was a dirt road leading to the Kentzingers farm house. As long as you walked that road to the farm house, everything was fine, but one thing we all knew, old Andy didn't like people walking on his property. So he planted a lot of corn, around the perimeter of the farm. Inside this perimeter he had a vegetable garden a vegetable stand and a large barn behind the house.

If you walked straight back, and around the house to the vegetable stand and bought what you needed and then walked back the way you came, everything was fine. When they got to know you especially Fannie we felt more at ease. We never saw much of old Andy in the later years.

Around 1935 when we still lived at 5th and Chester Ave. out by the AA Field, a silver Navy bye plane landed in Kentzinger's field. It was in the fall and the crops were gone. The Navy pilot was from Willow Grove air station, and had run out of fuel. Before he could get out of the plane, Andy was heading across the field with his double barrel shot gun. We were standing in front of our house, watching this whole event take place.

The pilot had convinced Andy that he had radioed for fuel, so Andy went back to the house and soon a truck came with the fuel. It wasn't long before the pilot taxied to the back of the field, turned around and headed straight toward River Road. As he lifted off he went right over Raphael and Johnson's garage, heading toward the Delaware River, and soon he was gone. It was something I'll always remember.

When Andy passed away, the farm was left to his daughter, Fannie. She kept it going for a few years and when she passed away, the property was willed to the Episcopal Church. They didn't want to build here because of the train, by the name of Nellie Blye that would barrel through here at 60 miles an hour spewing smoke and cinders along the way. I can still remember my grandmother closing the windows just before the train came by.

This good size piece of property sat empty for a number of years, and then the ACME came in and built a store on the corner of Front St. and Chester Avenue. Attached to the ACME was a dry cleaner and Johns Bargain Store, they all faced Chester Avenue. On this same side at 2nd Street was a garage owned and operated by Toni Mongo. A new bowling alley came in and took the name of Riverside Lanes, and the little garage on the corner became Cumberland Farms.

Over on the west side, next to Brown and Front Street, a few young men started a little league baseball team which I talked about earlier. Then a book supply company by the name of McMillan & Collier now Simon and Schuster moved in about 1960, and the baseball field had to go. Simon and Schuster are still expanding as I write. Then on the opposite side of Brown Street Joe Astroski Jr. and his wife Ann opened up a luncheonette where they served Hoagies, Steak Sandwiches, Pizza, soda, and a good size lunch meat counter. Their house was next to the store here on Brown Street. When Joe's health got bad he could no longer work, so Ann kept the store going until the children took over. After a number of years the business was sold, and today it is still operating under the name of BELLA.

Part 15

Rt.130

Now let's take a ride on Rt.130 starting at the Rancocus Creek and the Bridgeboro Bridge which is now a new overpass since 1984. We want to be at the southbound side of Rt. 130 starting in the area that is now Home Depot. This is where Lester Fortnum and his family lived, in the house next to the Rancocus Creek. His business, Fortnum Motors was located between his house and Yee-old Bridgeboro Inn. His showroom faced Rt.130 and it seems to me the garages in the back wrapped around Yee Old Bridgeboro Inn, and came out onto Bridgeboro Street. If you were coming from Riverside on Bridgeboro Street, you could go in and around the back of Yee Old Bridgeboro Inn, to Fortnum Motors service department. Harley Hankins worked there as a Ford mechanic. I don't know if you had to be a certified Ford mechanic or not, but the Hankins Boys were great mechanics. Lester also sold Oldsmobile's.

Yee-Old Bridgeboro Inn was a two story building with rooms on the second floor, and downstairs a bar and a dining room. Later in the 60's, it became Lancers Lounge. It was popular for many years until the State decided to demolish the old bridge, which had to be opened and closed to allow pleasure boats to pass through. It was replaced in 1984 with an arced overpass that was built high enough to allow boats to travel underneath. This overpass with its clover leaf and ramps, required a lot of land, and so these buildings had to go, "namely" Fortnum Motors, their house, Yee Old Bridgeboro Inn, which was Lancers Lounge at the time, Burdy's, Hammersley's, the Billboard, and that was only on the south side of Rt. 130.

Burdy's Beef and Ale House, (Bur'szt'yn'ski). Burdy's was another popular Tavern that sat back from Rt.130 on the opposite side of Bridgeboro St. The main entrance was on the side with a parking lot in the back, and inside a large square bar with the kitchen in the back. There were also a few tables along the front wall. This place was packed on the weekend, They had good food and on Saturday night, you would always see Burdy behind the bar serving drinks. When the tables were filled, and the people were eating, Burdy would bring out his violin, and play some sweet dinner music. The home town people loved it.

During the 40's, there was a service station on the corner, with an apartment on the top floor belonging to Bill Hamersley. About 200 hundred feet from Hamersley on Rt.130, was a large Billboard advertising Schlitz, or some other kind of beer. There was a lot of land between this billboard and the Delrando Diner. This diner was a favorite place to eat, for at least 10 or 15 years and then they packed up and left town. These type diners were always taken apart and shipped to a new location; I could probably look it up or find it somewhere in New Jersey, but what's the use.

Barlow Chevrolet opened a car sales business here on the corner of Fairview and Rt.130 in 1971, and next to Barlow was Paul Canton's Village Ford Sales which was sold to Delran Ford. This business went downhill also. In time Barlow bought them out and added box trucks to his business. He has quite a large inventory and is doing well at the present time.

This area from Fairview Street and very close to the Trinity Episcopal Church was originally the Lippincott family property. Jim Lippincott owned and operated Lippincott's Fuel Oil Co. on the corner of Fairview St. and Rt. 130. Jim Sr. was well known here in Delran. I remember him from back in the 40's, when he was a one man operation.

There were no automatic delivery systems back then; you'd just pick up the phone and call. Soon a truck would pull up and the door would open, and Jimmie Lippincott would step out. Yes, everyone called him

Jimmie. Now let me see if I can portray a picture of this man. He was fairly tall, medium weight, with a stubby cigar he held between his teeth. He had a smile that was infectious, and a manner that made your day.

It's great when people leave these good impressions for us to hold onto. The Lippincott home is still here in Fairview, and is occupied by Jimmie Lippincott Jr. and his wife Barbara (Hamlin) Lippincott who is my second cousin.

This side of Rt.130 has been known as the Fairview section of Delran, which dates back to the founding of the Trinity Episcopal Church in 1846, their Sunday school opened in 1847. Two of its founders were from Philadelphia, Thomas Quick and Phillip C. Timings and at the time this was Cinnaminson Township. Behind this church, there's a cemetery which the church lays no claim to.

Now while searching through documents I came upon the name of the cemetery twice.

Then my wife Elaine, received a phone call from a friend and school mate, Nancy (Hamlin) Fuoco, she had information for my book. When I called Nancy, she said while going through some papers and some old keepsakes, she found this document that was left to her by her great-great grandmother Ellen C. Stansbury. It was a deed to a cemetery lot at the Fairview Cemetery in Delran, N.J. and signed by the Trustees of the Fairview Christian Church, on the 30th day of May 1895.

The Trustees were, Wallace L. Gennett, George S. Bishop, and Lorenzo Wells. In 1833 a small wooden building with a cemetery a few years later, was built here on Rt. 130 and Fairview and at the time it was named, the Fairview Christian Meeting-House. At the time this area was prevalent with the Friends Society or Quakers as they were known, I'm sure this was their Meeting-House.

This Meeting-House was purchased on January the first 1842, and was fully organized April 14, 1845, by Rev. Samuel Hallowell Rector of the Episcopal Church at Beverly N.J. and became the Trinity Episcopal Church at Fairview. Here are some of the original members, Mrs. Julia Walton, Thomas Quick, Philip C. Timings, Ann T. Timings, John P. Bates and Wife, and John Cordingly.

Sam and Levi Abramowitz operated a scrap yard near the church, which is now Holy Cross High School property. They had some time dealing with Mr. Abramowitz on the sale of his property. They had been here so long that it was hard for them to give up the business; they had parts and pieces of farm machinery, wagons, tractors, and some scrap metal, and a small country store. They had an office and one of the few telephone booths in the area. People who lived here would walk to the Abramowitz office to make a phone call. Sam & Levi finally sold out to Holy Cross High School and moved on.

On the corner of Chester Ave. & Rt.130, there was the Delran Motor Court. This property stayed dormant for a few years. This motor court was built at a time when Rt. 130 was the main corridor from Philadelphia to New York, and business was good. But then Rt. 295 was completed in a very short time which put the Delran Motor Court out of business.

On the opposite corner of Chester Ave. was the famous Millside Farms, which started out as a partnership between Lashlocky and Kendal. In time Lashlocky bought out Kendal and I think the Kendal family worked for Millside Farms and had property back where the Municipal building is located today. Steven Lashlocky owned about 100 acres of ground at that time.

This was a large Dairy Farm with its bottling plant and ice house, a number of milkmen and trucks that delivered milk daily to the Riverfront communities. I worked for Steven Lashlocky during the summer months, like many others from this area. He was a good guy to work for and always paid well. His son Emory lost his life in France during the early part of the Second World War. Yes, another Delran boy who gave his all, for our Freedom.

The next farm belonged to the Eppolite family. This was mostly a vegetable farm with some fruit trees. On the front of the property they had a car repair shop that was operated by Fury Forcella. He married Samuel Eppolite's daughter. There is still a garage here on Rt.130 I wonder if it's the original Eppolite Garage.

Jochim's Chicken Farm was popular in the 40's. It was large and had these long chicken coops with the Leg Horn chickens that produced hundreds of eggs. He also raised chickens they called fryers, and if you had a chicken coop in your back yard, you could buy young leg horn chickens which laid nice white eggs. There were also Rhode Island reds that laid brown eggs. There was also a large apple orchard that was fenced off where Jack Nauss and John Steedle could go rabbit hunting that is with Mr. Jockim's permission. There were three guys from Riverside Park that worked for Mr. Jochem, Jack Nauss, Bob Heck, Jack Esworthy, and Carroll Kozianowski who was from Cambridge.

At certain times when there were lots of chickens hatching, Mr. Jochem would hire Japanese inspectors to sort out the female chicks from the male chicks. The male is a Cockerel and the female is a pullet. The Japanese inspectors could separate these birds within a margin of 99%. Mr. Jochem would call them in every so often to inspect the chicks, and they always did a fabulous job.

Wedeman's Farm was the last farm between Jockem's and Taylors Lane. This was another vegetable farm, with a cherry tree orchard in the back of the property. These entire farms looked for school kids to pick fruits and vegetables during the summer. They always paid by the basket, box, or crate, and the standard price was the same, no matter what farm you worked for.

Part 16

Bridgeboro

Let's go over to the northbound lane of Rt. 130 here at Taylor's Lane and travel to the Bridgeboro Bridge. Now again we have another one of the Eppolite farms, and along side of that was the Armstrong pasture and horse farm. Then on this side of Rt. 25, now Rt.130, Millside farm had its grazing ground. In the morning, the men who worked here would stop the traffic on both sides of the highway, and lead the cows from the barns over to the grazing grounds, which was all fenced off with two large gates. In the afternoon they would repeat the same operation bringing the cows back to the barns.

Next we come to Haines Mill Rd. and Chester Ave. jug handle, which was put in around 1950. Next to the jug handle a coal yard belonging to Van Owen & Denneler. This building is now occupied by ABC building materials. In the late 40's Joe Denneler bought Van Owens share of the business. It seems like this happened quite often with small business partners; they say it takes two to tango but then the music starts to fade and the dance is over. Joe continued on for a number of years not only with coal deliveries but also adding fuel oil trucks to the fleet.

In the back of this property was a farm belonging to the Cotton family, which I talked about earlier. To the left-hand side of the coal yard was a small piece of ground and then the Denneler's homestead which is gone now. Joe lived here for a number of years and later moved to the

Cambridge section of Delran. In the days when I played music in the clubs around town, I would meet Joe and his wife, Mildred, they loved to dance. Joe was one of those outgoing type guys and with a wife that was very attractive. They were just a pleasure to be around. Joe never failed to remember me from the days when we helped Lewie Anderson become a truck driver.

Joe's father owned a service station next to the house, with an office large enough for a desk on one side and a pool table on the other. Lewie and I would hang out there in the evenings and shoot pool, that's another thing Lewie could do, and do it well. I remember Joe Denneler's sister, Cass, coming in and challenging Lewie in a game of pool, they were both competitors. They played for 25 cents a game. The winner always called for another game but the loser usually had deep pockets and just couldn't find another quarter.

Roy Hulling's owned a Beer Distributer Company on the corner of Rt.25 and Hartford Rd. which is now owned by Canals wine and liquor. Roy had a number of garages in the back of the main building; they could have been used as horse stables at an earlier time, and then converted into garages. Roy Hullings loved the horses and could be found at the Garden State Race Track on numerous occasions. He was friends with the Zebrowski boys and could name the jockeys, the horses, and their breeders. This was their lifelong hobby. I guess everyone needs a hobby or two.

The Wills Farm Market was next. Howard Wills was my mother's uncle and as kids we always called him "Uncle Howard" and his wife was Aunt Agnes. As I mentioned before, my father built this market which back at that time was one of the many Farm Markets along Rt. 25. Howard owned a large piece of property in back of the farm market, his house sat to the right of the Farm Market. In the back of this property he built houses for each one of his children.

Here is a complete list of the family from the oldest to the youngest, Agnes, Iva, Evelyn, Mildred, Janet, Howard Jr. and Roland. They lost a young daughter Florence to a childhood disease long before they moved to Bridgeboro. My mother took me to the viewing at their house on the corner of Heullings and Washington St. in Riverside. It was sad and it left a mark, for every time I go past that house I think of Florence.

Let's get back to the Farm Market After a number of years Howard sold the front part of this property to Amoco for a gas station, and now it's a BP station and a car wash service. There is still a small road leading back to the houses which we called "Wellsville." A few of my cousins still live there.

Next, Frankie Hankins had an auto repair shop. He got his reputation back in the 30's working on model "A" and model "B" Fords. We had a model B Ford fire truck at the Riverside Park firehouse. When the engine needed a tune-up, we would call Frankie Hankins. As time went on, he taught other members of the fire company how to work on Fords. One of Frankie's longtime employees was Johnny Gasparto. He married Agnes Wills, and she was the oldest sibling of the Wills family. John is 92 and is living at the Lutheran home as I write, he is still self sufficient and has a memory like you wouldn't believe.

Now, coming closer to the bridge on Rt. 130, we find The Rite Spot. A little diner owned and operated by Joe Wigmore. He was a cook in the US Army during WWII and when he came home he had one thought in mind, and that was to open up a restaurant. His brother, Frank, was also in the Army. Their mother had a store in the front of her house on Cleveland Ave. in Riverside. These people were born business minded people through and through. I can remember as a young kid going into Mrs. Wigmore's store to buy candy, She always had patience with us even though we were only spending pennies. I guess that's why we called them Mom & Pop stores; they were so friendly with everyone. "The Rite Spot" seemed to be a family venture at that time.

After The Rite Spot, we come to Creek Road on the way to Bridgeboro Street, or Main Street as it was known at the time. There were a few more businesses along this part of Rt. 25. There was the Studebaker Car Sales, Barney Denney's Truck Co., and as we came to the Bridge there was Stein's Diner and the Red Mans Hall. This is where we turn right onto Main Street. Now we're in the business section. On the left you could see Marrazzo's Concrete Block Co. and Jim Lang's Barber Shop, Shimbach's Butcher shop, the US Post Office, Gotlieb Ziegler's Bakery

and Lang & Langden Insurance. Part way along Main on the left we find Cleveland Ave. and the Bridgeboro Fire Co. #1. George Merrills' Garage, John Knights' General store, George Heatons' Wagon Builder, and on the right, the United Methodist Church.

A few houses and then on the corner of Main and Creek Road was Flag's Nursery.

Now this becomes Bridgeboro Road and continues over to Moorestown. There was also Charlie Kauderers Bus Service, (Driver Cliff Newkirk) Kauderer ran a bus service from Bridgeboro, to the large grocery stores and banks in Riverside, and also bused school children in Riverside. There was a small farm here on Bridgeboro Rd. that belonged to Harry Beck who worked for the Township. He was the official garbage/trash man who started with a horse and wagon, and later a small dump truck. I remember him in the early days with the horse and wagon. This horse was so well trained that when Becky stopped to empty a trash can, the horse would stop, and when Becky started to walk to the next house the horse would start to walk. I guess as a young kid I was fascinated with Harry and his horse, so here's a little poem I wrote about my old friend Harry Beck.

> Here's a story of a man named Beck
> Who came to town one day
> He wore a hat and a pair of boots
> And his clothes were of disarray
> We thought his job was meaningless
> For taking but the trash
> But then we saw him dumping cans
> Of coal that burnt to ash
> And later on these metal cans
> That held the kitchen peels
> Were lifted up above his head
> And dumped without reveal

He had but yes a horse and cart
That took him all through town
And then with all his pickups done
His horse was homeward bound
There's not enough that I can say
About this man of fame
He had to turn around for home
Yes home from whence he came
Do you think recycling
Is something bright and new
Well here was our own Harry Beck
With process tried and true
He separated ash from peel
And also papers too
He also knew recycling
Was really over due
He paved the way for all of us
To treat the earth with good
So this is Becky's legacy
For all of us we should.

Let's go back to Creek Rd. and travel over to Moorestown, on the way we pass the Aaronson Bell Elementary School on the right, and a few houses on the left. This school has been demolished and a new school has been built as a replacement, which is Delran Intermediate School. I've been looking at the face of this building, for the name Aaronson Bell. He was one of the most important educators of our time. If his name is not on this building it should be. Now we come to the intersection at Main St. heading toward the farms.

The Andersons Peach Farm has been here since the 1800's. Their first farm was located in Willingboro across the Rancocas Creek from the present farm in Delran. When I talked with Ray a few years ago, he said that when the family moved over from Willingboro, they brought some of the farm equipment across the Rancocas Creek on barges. It seems to me this farm was always known as the Anderson Peach Farm. Then one day they built a roadside stand on the front of their property at Creek road, and named it Rainbow Meadow Farm.

In the early days they built dikes sometimes known as flood gates, along the banks of the Rancocas creek. This was a way to control the flood waters for their crops, which were mostly celery and lettuce. The farm was fairly small in the beginning only 23 acres. Then, after WWII, Ray acquired additional acreage next to his farm, which increased the farms acreage to over 100 acres.

In the 40's they increased the farms output of vegetables, and then they started to plant peach trees. By 1960 this farm became a peach farm with about 12,000 peach trees, from Creek Road, all the way down to the Rancocas Creek. They also joined the New Jersey Fruit Coop, and grew only USDA grade #1 peaches. In the early 40's, a few of the guys from "The Park" including myself, would earn money picking peaches at Andersons. The farm was still relatively small, but continuing to grow. I think they were still growing lettuce at the time.

We worked a few hours early in the day climbing ladders and picking peaches. The one important thing I still remember was to keep my shirt buttoned up, including my collar, and to always wear a scarf around my neck. If you've ever had peach fuss around your neck, you would know what I mean, it never stops itching. I think some parents used the peach farm as a deterrent. If a child was unruly the parents would say I'm sending you to pick peaches! I know for a fact that some kids from our neighborhood refused to work on a peach farm.

A friend and neighbor of mine namely Bill Pfeffer, worked for the Andersons, and when I interviewed him he said he had worked in the packing house. We pickers always said the packing house was made for the privileged, that is, the pickers were out in the hot sun, while the packers were in the cool packing house. My friend, Bill, took exception to this rationale, he fired back by saying, this packing house was all hard work. It had a number of conveyors, tables and crates, and also a large washer and at one end there was a large freezer.

He also said there were several work stations along the conveyor belts, where the workers would remove the defective and overripe peaches. Then there were three work stations were the peaches were placed in crates, each crate had to weigh 38 pounds. The inspectors would switch peaches of different sizes to make sure each crate was of the proper weight. Then the peaches were off to the washer, and then into the freezer. This freezer could hold approximately 1,000 crates of peaches. They were stored here until the tractors and trailers arrived. Once the trailers were loaded the day's work was done. The Andersons produced about 25,000 boxes of peaches a year, each box weighing 38 pounds.

Bill said that picking peaches was important but once they were picked, they had to be sorted, washed, and weighed and then, sent to the freezer as fast as possible. I never gave it a thought but peaches have to be picked and shipped to market, before they get overripe. He also talked about working at the Lippincott farm, planting tomato plants. I also worked at this same farm, suckering corn. If you don't know what suckering corn means, I'll try to explain.

Corn is planted in rows spaced about 20 inches apart. When the stokes grow to a certain height there's always smaller stokes around the bottom, these are called "suckers" and they must be removed. This was a job for the young boys. The process was to get down on your hands and knees, and crawl along each row pulling these suckers out by the roots. If you looked down one row, you could just about make out the very end, and you were paid to remove these suckers by the row. So to make any money you had to move down to the end of the row quickly, and then move to the next row. One or two hours of this was enough for a day.

There were a few houses and farms along the way to the Moorestown border. This is the area where John Hollinshead was one of the pioneers who bought 550 acres of land along the Rancocas Creek in 1678. The land became known as the "Hollinshead Dock" which was a little below the Burlington and Salem road built in 1682. The Hollinshead Ferry was running by the early 1700's. If you go out Creek Road close to Moorestown you should look for Cox Road on your right, this is the exact place where the Hollinshead Ferry crossed the Racocas Creek over to Willingboro.

From Delran's beginning up to the Second World War, Bridgeboro had the largest acreage of farm land in Delran. If we look at the map, we can see how the roads were configured over the years. You can see Bridgebro Rd continued from Main St. over to Moorestown. Then Hartford Rd. from Rt. 130 to Moorestown, and Haines Mill Rd. from Rt. 130 over to Bridgeboro Rd. and last we have Conrow Rd.which crosses between Hartford and Haines Mill Rd. Now, let's see if we can find something significant about each one of these roads. For example the Anderson peach farm and the Lippincott vegetable farm and the Lamb's Farm were part of the land that once belonged to the Hollinshead's. This was then Chester Township.

Now as Main St. changes to Bridgeboro Rd. the first business was Flagg's Nursery, in time they moved out closer to Moorestown and are still in business. Now let's look at Hartford Rd. Here again we have lots of farms, but at the cross roads of Bridgeboro and Hartford there's Ott's Tavern, which used to be Ott's farm.

In the early days Delran had no police force. The Ott family had one or two sons who were N.J. State Police officers who would patrol the area. They even had their own patrol car stationed at the farm.

As you travel over to Moorestown you'll notice a well built Foot Bridge on the right just before you come to Borton Landing Rd. This is where Swedes Run continues over through Moosetown.

We still have Haines Mill Rd, a very famous road. In the 1750's there was a grist mill here that belonged to the Borton family, they later sold this to the Haines family whose house still stands today. As you leave Rt.130 onto Haines Mill Rd. you'll see Millside Shopping Center on your right, and to the left a gas station. Then a gray two story building which was the Haines family home. The grist mill was in the back of the property.

It's a short run from Haines Mill Rd. to Moorestown, this was also farm land. When you get to the water tank, you'll come to Conrow Road, which travels over to Hartford Rd. This road was named after the Conrow family; their house was built in 1751 and has since been demolished to make way for the Delran Millbridge School. Around 1940, Delran farmers owned about 2000 acres of land in this area.

A few notes before I close. Historians, including myself, write about people and things as they were. This gives us a prospective between the past and the present and what the future may hold for us. Then we make predictions in our own little way. So if you don't mind, my prediction for the future looks great, I may even say overwhelmingly spectacular.

The Industrial Revolution is over; the Space Race is doing fine, and now we're on our way to win the Information Revolution. How much better can things get? Well let me remind you again about my neighbors on Alden Ave. back in the 1930,s and continuing into the 70,s peaking away at that "glass ceiling."

First Peg (Jenkins) Wigmore who played on the first women's basketball team at Glassboro College in the 1930's, and then her daughter Lorraine (Wigmore) Schmeirer who became the first elected and the longest running Mayor of Delran in the 1970's. And soon, the United State of America may have a women president. Believe me the glass ceiling is just about gone forever and the future has never looked brighter. Finally, God made (Anecdotist) out of all mankind by giving each and every one of us a conscience, and so I leave you with one more poem I wrote just in case you've lost your way.

The Anecdotist

Listen to your conscience ... And try to do no wrong

Take this with you everyday ... And life will make you strong

Keep a smile within your heart ... For everyone you meet

And let this be the anecdote ...That makes your life complete.

Acknowledgements

I like to thank the Burlington County Library and the staff for information on the early days of Delran Township, and also Scott Homan of the Cinnaminson Library, The cooperation of Mayor Paris and various people at the Delran Municipal Building, namely, Jeff Hatcher, Joanne (Rosati) Fenimore, Sandy (Stellwag) Craft. Richard Grockenberger, President of the Delran Senior Citizens Club. Dianne & Yosh Dudek, Regina Collinsgru of the Positive Press, Bob Kenney, Louis Camishion for information on Hollingshead Ferry, Dorothy Bart, John Steedle, Eli (Wink) McCarter Jr. Joann (McCarter) Dallman, Dave Dallman, Charlie Shinn Jr. Shirley Woodington, Fred George & Bill Pfeffer, Ruth Lipinski, Carroll Kozianowski, George Myers, Bill Parsons Sr. John & Frank Wigmore, Fred Wolff Jr. Jane Maher, Paul Ackerman, Bill Breuer, Charlie Forcell Howard Rendfrey, Bob & Connie Townsend, Emily Wills, Lorraine Schmeirer, Fran Zeisweiss, Thanks to Nancy & Carmen Fuoco, Barbara & Jim Lippincott, and Don Shafer on the Fairview section. Thanks for additional Photos from Dorothy Bart, Fran & Wayne Klingler, Bob Knoll, and Charlie Shinn Jr. Cindy Wasco, thanks to my promotional team Tim & Mike Wasco, Thanks to my Editors William Pfeffer Chief Editor & Thomas Winkelspek. And my proof reader Dianne Dudek and a special thanks to Robert Heck for without his encouragement and his Knowledge of this area, this book would not be possible.

Made in the USA
Thornton, CO
12/23/24 19:05:20

81185f8e-72a6-4174-9e7a-d0efe925f952R01